LIGHT UP
YOUR LIFE

DIANA COOPER

LIGHT UP YOUR LIFE

DISCOVER YOUR TRUE PURPOSE AND POTENTIAL

PIATKUS

For more information on other books published by Piatkus, visit our website at www.piatkus.co.uk

© 1991 Diana Cooper

First published in 1991 by
Ashgrove Press Limited, Bath, Avon

This edition first published in 1995 by
Judy Piatkus (Publishers) Ltd of
5 Windmill Street, London W1T 2JA
email: info@piatkus.co.uk

Reprinted 1996, 1998, 1999 (twice), 2000 (twice), 2001

**The moral rights of the author
have been asserted**

*A catalogue record for this book is
available from the British Library*

ISBN 0-7499-1986-8 pb

Printed and bound in Great Britain by Biddles Ltd
www.biddles.co.uk

CONTENTS

chapter   *page*

ONE   We Create Our Lives   9
TWO   The Power of Our Thoughts   14
THREE   The Law of Attraction   21
FOUR   How We Are Programmed   28
FIVE   Life Choices   35
SIX   Love and Fear   43
SEVEN   The Law of Cause and Effect   52
EIGHT   Anger   58
NINE   Creating Our Reality   64
TEN   The Inner Child   72
ELEVEN   Healing the Wounded Child   79
TWELVE   The Healing Power of Forgiveness   86
THIRTEEN   Healing Relationships   93
FOURTEEN   The Heart Centre   99
FIFTEEN   Balance   107
SIXTEEN   The Body is a Reflection of the Mind   114
SEVENTEEN   Soul Choices   123
EIGHTEEN   Images and Symbols   130
NINETEEN   Dreams   138
TWENTY   Releasing Negative Ties   146
TWENTY-ONE   Responsibility   155
TWENTY-TWO   Depression   163
TWENTY-THREE   Images and Affirmations   173
TWENTY-FOUR   Love and Light   180

With love
To Eric, Cheryl, Lorraine and Justin

ONE

We Create Our Lives

It was one of those sunny spring days when it feels good to be alive and I breathed in the fragrant air as I watched Chris jump into her car.

Her smile and wave were full of life and the bump of the baby she was expecting clearly showed under her dress.

I could picture the Chris who strode through my gate for her first appointment a year before. She had short dark curly hair and a purposeful gait. She walked rigidly without any flow in her body and nodded when she saw me, no trace of a smile.

In those days Chris carried her own personal thundercloud with her and had done so most of her life.

She eyed me warily as she sat in the chair in my office. Her voice was tense and sharp as she started to tell me about herself.

She told me bitterly that her mother was only interested in clothes and had no affection for her. Her father was always working and interested only in money and success. He was excessively mean and begrudged her the money for College so that she had left without finishing her course. She wasn't going to feel beholden to him.

She didn't have time for their narrow way of life and she hardly ever saw them.

As a child she had always felt different, shy and awkward. At school she had been bullied unmercifully and no one seemed to notice or protect her.

She'd failed most of her exams, even though she was intelligent, because no one encouraged her.

She wanted to do something with her life and here she

was, stuck in a dead end job working for boring people and there was nothing she could do about it. Her frustration was enormous.

All her life she had been unlucky. Nothing good came her way. She used to try to please people but it was no good. They didn't respond and she felt no one liked her.

The only good thing in her life was her boy friend. They lived together now and he felt exactly as she did. Life was a grim battle and held nothing for them.

They had no money and couldn't even afford a car. Anyway it wouldn't make any difference if they could because she didn't have the confidence to drive.

She'd never get married she informed me. It was much too dangerous. And she'd certainly never bring a baby into this terrible world.

'There was nothing anyone could do was there?' her eyes said accusingly as she sat back, crossing her arms and glowering. Yet behind the frowning, accusing façade, there was a desperate, fearful appeal. She looked lost and alone. I couldn't help but remember myself in the days when I felt I was a helpless victim of fate. Life seemed so threatening.

I took Chris through her life, showing her exactly how she had made these difficult relationships and events happen. I explained the Laws of the Universe.

The Laws of the Universe are the great Laws by which we live. They govern our lives, for we are in a structured Universe, subject to Spiritual Laws. By these Laws we attract all the people and situations to us. When we understand and apply them we can take responsibility for ourselves and give our lives direction and purpose. Then we leave behind the role of helpless victim and our lives transform.

Chris accepted and applied the Laws and within a year she had a creative job which she loved. She and her boyfriend had married and she was expecting a baby.

She had healed her relationship with her parents and her father had bought her a car which she had learnt to drive.

Her body moved with vitality and energy and her face was expressive and alive. Her life was happy and she had the tools and knowledge to keep it that way.

People generally are becoming more aware that there is structure in the Universe but are not sure what it is or how to apply it.

The more understanding we have, the easier our journey towards wholeness and happiness becomes. We then no longer allow ourselves to be victims of fate.

This book is about the Laws of the Universe and how we can take responsibility and use them to create the life we want. It illustrates that there is no such thing as chance or bad luck or good luck or accidents. We do not live in a haphazard world.

The Laws of the Universe are exact and when we understand and apply them properly, peace, love, health, prosperity and success must follow.

When we believe that we are helpless and that people or circumstances can do things to us, we are victims. Because we feel powerless to take responsibility for what is happening inside ourselves, we blame outside factors.

We blame people for hurting us. We blame the Government or the education system for our unsatisfactory job. We blame our parents for our lack of confidence. We blame fate for our life circumstances.

When we understand how and why we are in our current circumstances we can learn how to become masters of our destiny.

The quality of our lives comes from within us. It is within the capacity of all of us to create wonderful lives. We can dissolve the pain, hurts and fears which cause our problems and experience the life we desire.

The turning point comes when we accept that we are responsible for everything in our lives.

When we take responsibility for what is happening around us we recognise that life is a reflection of what is happening in our minds. Then we ask how we have attracted or created that difficult situation or unhappy relationship or ill health. We can then take steps to change or heal it. If we look at a tree reflected in a lake, we may see a broken branch or that it needs pruning. We realise that there is no point in trying to change the reflection, so we turn to the tree and neatly saw the broken branch. We prune the excess growth. Then the reflection will also change.

So it is in our lives.

For over forty years of my life I believed that I had to take whatever fate handed to me. I did not know that I personally am responsible for creating my life and that life gives me what I cause it to give me.

All those years I was a victim because I didn't know how to take responsibility for myself.

I used to be a tense anxious person who often felt depressed and very unsafe in a huge, hostile world. I often felt guilty and helpless and very angry. I found it very frightening to believe I was a powerless victim of fate.

When I met new people I wasn't sure if they would like me, so I either clammed up or put a lot of effort into being very pleasant.

When it came to trying new things, I'd either not do it in case I failed or else I'd work very hard to make absolutely sure I succeeded.

Inside me there was a very hurt, undervalued part which I hid from the world. Like so many people I'd learnt as a child that only the competent, smiling side of me was acceptable.

Those hurt, inadequate, angry, jealous feelings, I pushed deep down inside me. I covered them up with tight control and often with alcohol or constant eating, so that I could present a coping façade to the world. It used a lot of energy.

It was not until my life fell completely to pieces that I was forced to look at the way the Universe works, the purpose of Life and why we are in the life situations we are in. Most important I learnt how we can take mastery, so that we can fulfil our destiny.

Since that time I have been on the most exciting, amazing voyage of discovery. Now I know who I am, why I am here, where I am going. I still constantly trip and fall but the knowledge and understanding mean I can pick myself up and carry on.

I hope that by sharing some of my experiences and learnings and those of my clients and friends with you, your life will be happier and easier.

This book shows us how our life changes as we change our inner beliefs. Everything in our life is a clear reflection of what we believe.

One of the Spiritual Laws says, As within, so without. When we learn how to dissolve our negative beliefs and fears and allow the positive to emerge, our lives change.

I offer you this book with love to light up your life and help you on your pathway.

TWO

The Power of Our Thoughts

Joe was a thin anxious man and a terrible worrier. He worried about lack of money and he constantly pictured the outcome of not having enough.

As a child he had experienced poverty. He vividly recalled a time when he was ten years old. His mother had no money and the electricity was cut off. The awful darkness and cold made a deep impression on him and he constantly replayed this and other scenes of poverty in his mind.

He came to see me because he felt under such stress. Recently he had forgotten again and again to pay his electricity bill until it was cut off. Then he lost his wallet so he was indeed short of money. The fear that everything would be taken from him preyed on his mind and he thought he might lose his job as he was no longer able to cope. He kept imagining his boss handing him his notice and all the consequences.

Joe had no idea why he had forgotten again and again to pay the electricity bill. He was angry with himself. He thought he was unlucky to lose his wallet. He felt powerless to change his situation at work.

He had no idea he was responsible for all that was happening. He didn't know that he had set in train the greatest power on earth, the power of his thoughts.

Our thoughts are so powerful that when we focus them onto something we set in motion mighty forces, which eventually make our vision happen.

Our thoughts and beliefs are conscious, so our conscious mind controls our life.

If we kept every thought, feeling and experience at the level of awareness, we would suffer from overload, so we store information in our inner mind, which is our computer or memory bank.

The way we give instructions to our inner mind is with our thoughts. These thoughts form pictures. The more powerful and vivid our thoughts, the clearer the picture we give our mind of what we want it to do. It will then do what we tell it to.

It works like this. Say you are playing golf and your ball lands in front of the bunker. If you think, 'I bet that ball goes into the bunker,' you picture for an instant the ball in the bunker.

Your inner computer receives the picture, believes it has been given an instruction and puts the ball in the bunker for you. The more energy you put into the thought, the more likely it is to work for you.

All top golfers will mentally picture the ball landing where they want it to before they swing.

The Law says, 'We are what we think.' Joe believed he was a poor failure and thought accordingly. All day long he was picturing poverty and lack, so he was telling his mind to find ways to create poverty. Joe, who thought he was powerless, was succeeding very powerfully in carrying out his own instructions.

He was also selectively accessing memories of poverty. It transpired that there had been times of financial stability but, by focusing on the bad times, his belief was that he was powerless to be other than poor. He saw his past as unremittingly poor and believed in lack and loss. It was time for Joe to re-educate his beliefs about money and start to build up his good qualities by putting new instructions into his inner mind. We started to put in pictures of success for him and he fed those instructions with constant thoughts and expectations of good things happening.

As he concentrated on the positive pictures, his inner confidence grew and he started to have faith that he could succeed in life. All the power he had been putting into failing he now put into succeeding.

A few months later he was on top of his job again and was promoted.

We store everything in our inner minds. Here we record everything we see and hear and remember what needs to be done. Joe's inner mind knew he had to pay the electricity bill and would normally send a reminder through to his conscious awareness but he counter-manded the reminder with powerful thought instructions that the electricity was to be cut off.

If we lose or forget something, if we fail to see or hear something, it is because we have decided at an inner level not to. Our thoughts create what happens in our lives and, because every thought is an instruction to which our mind responds, we can use our thoughts to create what we want to happen. It applies to every area of our lives.

If a woman thinks her husband is going to be angry because she has ruined his best shirt, she starts to worry. As the worrying thoughts churn round in her mind, she imagines her husband getting angry.

She pictures him getting red in the face, grinding his teeth, tearing out his hair. She can probably imagine what he is saying.

She is putting a very powerful instruction into her inner mind. It has received a clear message to find ways to make her husband angry. Filed away in her memory banks are learnings on how to make a person angry, and more specifically, how to make her husband angry.

When she next sees him she will use the particular expression that annoys him, the words that rile him, the gesture that aggravates him and the tone of voice that gets under his skin, and she will trigger his anger. She says miserably to herself, 'He's so unreasonable. I knew he'd be angry', with no idea that she made it happen.

Waldo Emmerson said, 'Be careful of your thoughts for you may get them'.

Imagination can be our greatest gift or our worst enemy. The choice is ours. We can choose to picture disaster or success, illness or health, darkness or light, misery or happiness.

Worriers often have good imaginations. They are programmed by early experiences to see or expect the worst. If they clearly and constantly picture images of things going wrong in their lives, they make them go wrong.

Jane had an unsatisfactory relationship with her husband. They quarrelled a great deal and he was suspicious and untrusting. She blamed him for the state of the marriage. Whenever she came home late from work, they would row.

She poured out her anger about it to me and then we started to talk about her part in creating the situation at home. She didn't want to hear. She declared it was all his fault and as a victim it was more comfortable for her to blame her husband. As she drove home from my office she suddenly realised that she was already tensing up as she imagined the quarrel ahead.

She stopped the car and thought over what I'd explained about her thoughts. Then she sat for a while and imagined her husband happy and welcoming and pleased to see her.

At once she felt warmer and more friendly towards him and indeed when she arrived home in a warm, friendly mood, her husband responded affably and they enjoyed a happy evening.

Jane realised that whenever she was late she had gone home on the defensive and helped to create the bad atmosphere. That moment's awareness sowed the seed of a growth towards happiness in her marriage.

Victims blame others. As Jane stopped blaming and took responsibility for what she was doing the situation changed. Her husband was not suspicious of the open friendly Jane, only of the withdrawn, secretive, defensive person who came in late from work.

We all fear things. It can be anything from being afraid of being left alone, to being terrified an animal will bite us, to fearing being robbed. Each time we have a thought about it, we imprint the fear more deeply into our inner programme. So we are creating the belief or expectation that this fear will happen and our inner computer is looking for an opportunity to bring this about.

When we expect or believe something will happen, we make it happen.

Our thoughts are the seeds which create our lives. Our expectations water those seeds and ensure that they produce healthy plants. When we recognise that something has happened in our lives so somehow we are responsible for making it happen, we can start to look for the seed thoughts within us. Then we pull out the weeds and sow flower seeds instead.

So when an area of our life is not working for us we need to look for the thoughts we are sending out to make it not work.

A very elegant yet bitter lady came to see me. Her mouth was etched with tight lines. She had terrible digestive problems. She poured out her anger and rage and frustration.

Her teenage stepson had come to live with them. He was untidy, dirty, bad tempered and rude. He slammed doors and disrupted the house. She and her husband were quarrelling because of him. Her own children were angry and resentful of him.

'I just wish he'd go away and never come back again,' she said. 'I'd be happy if he'd disappear off the face of the earth. He's ruining my life. It's all his fault.'

When she calmed down she told me that he'd had a terrible life with his own mother who treated him like an animal.

So I asked her to close her eyes and imagine a puppy who had been beaten, kicked and abused and was so frightened that it growled and barked at or even bit the person who took it in.

She visualised herself patiently, quietly soothing and comforting the puppy – accepting and understanding the fear and lack of trust which made it growl. At last she saw in her imagination the puppy quieten and she was able to stroke it and begin to gain its trust.

I suggested she think of her stepson as that puppy whenever he was in the house. I asked her to think as many nice, loving thoughts about him as she could while he was at school.

She immediately volunteered a few nice things about his nature which she'd 'forgotten'. Then she added wryly, 'Perhaps if I didn't get angry and shout at him, he wouldn't slam doors'.

One week later she returned looking so much happier. She had acted on the suggestion to imagine her stepson as a hurt puppy and that made it easier to think kindly thoughts about him. Because of this he had let his hackles drop and was being much nicer. He no longer slammed doors.

Her digestion had improved.

She felt warmer towards her husband. They had become closer.

Her own children, who were no longer being bathed in her rage and fury became more friendly towards their stepbrother.

In one week, by changing her thoughts, she had begun a healing process which continued to spread.

Most people and all children are open and sensitive to atmospheres created by the thoughts of others. Because our thoughts affect others so profoundly, if we want a loving relationship with someone, we must think loving thoughts about that person.

If we want people to like us, think friendly thoughts about them. If we want our boss to give us a rise imagine it. If we worry that our child will do badly at school, he will pick up our expectations and fulfil them. So if we want our child to do well at school, we must think successful thoughts about him.

Imagination is our greatest gift. We can use it for ourselves and the Universe not against it. Please use it to create happiness. Visualize love and peace.

Our minds are very powerful. Let us use them to work for us. The difference between animals and humans is that we have the ability to control our thoughts. Most of us let our thoughts run riot and create havoc in our lives but when we move onto the Spiritual Path we take responsibility. That means we watch our thoughts and learn to master them. Then we become masters of our destiny.

Every thought we send out forms a picture which imprints like a photo on the ether. A single thought may dissolve but if we repeat a thought again and again with energy and strength, it becomes reality.

Castles are always created in the mind before they are put on paper, then built. So we must have castles in the air before we build them in reality.

When we hold a vision steadfastly, without doubt or deviation, it must be created.

THREE

The Law of Attraction

Every thought we have radiates around us, creating an energy field. Our energy fields, or auras, can now be photographed by Kirlian photography.

All thoughts have a colour. We know them instinctively – dark red with anger, green with jealousy, grey with misery and black with depression.

If we radiate loving thoughts, we radiate pink. Healing is blue and wisdom is golden.

Each and every one of us is a light bulb radiating our own individual light and colour. We can choose whether we radiate dark red anger or pink love, black misery or golden wisdom, murky green jealousy or an orange happiness.

What we radiate activates that same colour, feeling, energy or thought in others.

Therefore a courageous commander can inspire his troops to acts of courage, a genuine preacher radiating love and peace, activates those feelings in his congregation and can send everyone home feeling loving and peaceful.

Hitler triggered arrogance and hatred in millions. We know what happened.

Mother Theresa triggers devotion and selfless caring.

On a dark night when there seems no hope, a single light shining out can give strength, hope, courage and inspiration to thousands; and so can we as our inner light gets stronger and stronger.

I well recall some years ago when I had a crisis in my life and my mind was in turmoil, I stayed for a few days at a Healing Centre. There was only one other guest and I spoke very little during my stay but the warden and his wife radiated love and peace and I could feel it enfold me. The turmoil in my mind quietened, allowing me to think clearly. I returned home at peace, with new insights and with renewed strength to get through the crisis. In their quiet corner that man and wife were radiating a beautiful uplifting yet soothing light.

And thought power works on every level. I have never smoked. This means that I don't have the thought of tobacco in my mind. I have a friend who is a compulsive smoker. She says that the only time she can stop smoking is when she is staying with me.

Were I a smoker or ex-smoker, because she is sensitive she would be constantly picking up the thought of cigarettes from my mind and then her craving would be triggered.

We constantly transmit thoughts around us which activate other people's latent thoughts and feelings.

It is important to be aware of what we are transmitting. What we send out in thoughts, feelings, energy, colour, or however you feel most comfortable describing it, is what we attract into our lives.

Like attracts like. *Every person in our lives is there because we attracted them by something we radiated. This is the Law of Attraction. When we give out an energy it is like a magnet, attracting the same energy back into our lives.*

I remember when a friend had taken some decisions involving changes which meant I wouldn't see him so much. On one level I felt quite happy that this would give me time to do what I wanted. At a deeper level, which I suppressed, I felt angry, hurt and rejected.

A few days after the decision was taken I had a phone call from a lady I'd met a few months before. To put her at ease I told her I'd met her before at such and such an event with her husband and remembered her well. At that she launched into a stream of bitter invective about her husband. For twenty minutes she raged angrily about him.

Any petals of peace I tried to drop in were blown away on the winds of her wrath.

When I put the phone down I held her in healing thoughts for some time. Then I looked at what within me had attracted that blast into my life at that moment. Because only something within myself could have brought that woman's anger to me, I was forced to look honestly at what I was really feeling and thinking about the change in my relationship. When I acknowledged to myself the feelings of anger, hurt and rejection I was feeling, I was able to start the healing process.

Until we acknowledge to ourselves how we feel, we are not in a position to heal the underlying feelings.

Everything we give out comes back in some way. We can never give away love. It always comes back to us somehow. If we give money away with love, it must return in some form – perhaps as caring or friendship or a good deed.

If we give money away out of fear, we are not freely giving it. We are exchanging it. If we fear that the recipient won't like us unless we give him money, we are buying friendship. If we fear someone won't look after us unless we give money, we are exchanging money for the expectation of being looked after.

When two energies are exchanged, they cancel each other out. So if we give money to charity to appear a good person, we are exchanging money for the esteem of others. And if we are hoping to bargain with the Almighty by giving money away, we are exchanging hope for cash.

The important factor is the underlying feeling and intention with which we give money away.

If we feel we are always doing things for others and never get anything in return, we should check on our motivation. The Law is exact, as you give, so you receive.

It is so easy to mistake exchange for love. How common it is to say we love a child when we really mean, 'I value you as long as you are a credit to me'. In a relationship, the exchange often is, 'I will take care of you as long as you meet my needs,' or, 'I will support you emotionally if you will do the same for me'.

I can look back at my life and clearly see where I've

exchanged care, attention, support, money and many
other things in the mistaken belief I was giving love – and
I still find myself doing it, but I'm learning – and life is all
about learning.

Genuine love is given without expectation of return. It
is freely, unconditionally given. It is a total acceptance of a
person as he or she is.

And when we totally accept someone as they are, we
give them safety to grow and develop.

The Spiritual Law is exact. We receive in the measure
that we give.

And every situation in our life is a response to what we
are giving out. Every event is drawn to us by what we
give out, negative or positive.

Mick was nine when his parents' marriage started to
break down. He was a sensitive, anxious child, with large
dark eyes. No one said anything to him about the break-
down but he sensed that something awful was happening. In the six months before they finally told him that
they had decided to split up, Mick had three unrelated
accidents to his eyes. He felt angry, fearful, guilty and
resentful about what he was seeing in his life, so he
attracted accidents to his eyes.

As soon as his parents told him that they were separat-
ing and the situation was openly discussed, it was as if a
thundercloud was lifted from around him. He could see
what was going on, talk about it and he didn't need to
have accidents to his eyes any more.

Accidents are never accidental. Paul had spent his life
working for one company. His work was his life and he
gave the company his all. One day out of the blue he was
called in to his boss's office and told that he was being
made redundant. He came out of the office looking ashen.
The terms were reasonable and next morning he was
quite composed and told everyone he was happy and
positive about his retirement.

A week before he left, he had an accident in his
company car which cost several thousand pounds to
repair. The cost of the repair was an exact energy

exchange for the unacknowledged anger he was feeling, for money is an energy.

Each and every thought and feeling contributes to what we create and we are responsible for having made it happen.

Nothing happens by chance. There is no such thing as an accident.

A young man told me that he had borrowed his father's car without permission. As he drove it he was so worried that he could actually picture returning the car with a dent in the side.

It happened exactly as he imagined. 'You mean I made it happen?' he said, and his eyes widened as he became aware of the power latent in his thoughts.

His vivid worry picture had caused him to transmit a powerful message into the ether. This was picked up by someone with the same underlying fear and they collided.

If we imagine our mind is our personal computer it is easy to understand his message being relayed to the master computer which looks for someone sending out the thought energy for an accident and brings them together. They don't have to be sending out the message positively at that moment. It can have been stored away and accumulating. Nor do they both have to be active in the accident. It depends on the exact message they are sending out. One may be passively stationary when he is hit. But it has not happened by chance and the innocent one is not a victim.

Our thoughts draw experiences towards us from outside. Because like attracts like, we draw into our lives the people, events and situations most similar to what is going on within us.

Thus we attract what we need for our growth, not necessarily what we want to happen.

Have you ever noticed how often it is that the person who compulsively checks that every door and window is locked, is the one who is repeatedly burgled? His fear attracts the robbery.

We attract that which we fear most into our lives, in

order that we may learn what our fears are, face them, and master them.

As we dissolve our fears we clarify the colours we radiate, so we naturally help others to purify or strengthen their colours.

Lara's son refused to go to bed. He would come downstairs for a drink of water. Ten minutes later he would come down because he was afraid of the dark, and after that because he couldn't get to sleep and later still because he wanted to talk to her.

She became uptight, resentful, tired and felt she was a hopeless mother. The more hostile she felt towards him, the more demanding he became until she was at screaming point.

For many weeks she ignored my suggestion that she should relax twice a day and clearly visualise him going to bed easily. At length, she decided to try it. Twice a day she clearly imagined him going to bed, happy and relaxed and staying there. The rest of the time she made a determined effort to think positive things about him.

On the third evening he announced he was tired and went to bed without a murmur and again on the fourth. There were one or two setbacks but Lara created a new bedtime pattern with her thought power, and a happier life for herself and her son.

Lara's son had been responding to the anger and hostility she had been feeling towards him. Small wonder he had not felt safe to relax and go to sleep. He feared that such a hostile mother might abandon him. When she relaxed towards him, his fear abated and he was safe to go to bed and know she would be there for him in the morning.

Lara softened the ugly black and red she was sending to her son into a gentle pink. Naturally this affected him and the light he radiated softened too.

So as we change ourselves we automatically help others to radiate a clearer light.

We readily accept that dogs respond to our moods, our very thoughts. We know that a dog instinctively picks up a person's fear and responds accordingly.

When my son was three we moved house and I sent him on an errand to my new neighbour's house, totally forgetting that she had a huge German Shepherd dog with a reputation for viciousness. At that time we had never owned a dog nor really had contact with any.

My neighbour later described to me what happened. My little son walked through the gate, carefully carrying the dish he was returning for me, whereupon the dog, barking wildly, charged towards him.

Justin glanced up, smiled and said, 'Oh, do be quiet, Vera, and mind out of my way'. The huge, wolflike creature was so stunned that she fell back on her haunches in silence and stared at him.

He, in his child wisdom, responded to her torrent of fury with love. Because there was no fear response within him to feed her fury, it abated.

People respond in exactly the same way to the feelings of love that we give out. *Love abates fury.*

Yet there are people who are gentle, kind and peace loving who have violent things happen to them.

This is because there is a fear of violence or a deep anger within them, which attracts the violence. And it may be at a deep, unaware level. It may even be a lesson unlearned from another life. Their lesson now is to accept, acknowledge and face the fear, then they can release it and violence is no longer attracted to them.

Light attracts moths and as our inner light shines more and more brightly, darker situations and people come towards us. It is our opportunity to face our deepest shadows. The brighter the light the darker the shadow and the greater the opportunity for growth.

FOUR

How We Are Programmed

The Jesuits said, 'Give me a child until he is seven and I will give you the man.' They knew that we form our beliefs in these early years and after that we replay this programming unless we learn how to change it.

As babies, even in the womb, we are open and sensitive to the thoughts and feelings of anyone close to us. The impressions become stronger until they seem fact, and then we believe them. So we form our belief system.

When we are a sensitive baby or child what happens is not so important as the way we perceive it. That becomes our reality.

Michael's mother became pregnant with him soon after marriage. She was young and they had little money. Alone in a high rise block of flats she knew no one and each day stretched endlessly, depressingly ahead of her.

She often cried when her husband left her alone to go to work. As a baby Michael naturally picked up all her feelings. He perceived that it is frightening to be alone and also that he wasn't good enough to comfort his mother.

Whenever he cried his mother shut him in his room because her jangled nerves couldn't stand the noise. He felt rejected and this reinforced his belief that it was frightening to be alone. He could sense her rage and frustration when he cried and feared she would push him away. So he buried his needs and became quiet and withdrawn so that she wouldn't leave him alone.

As he grew older he tried harder to comfort his mother but of course the basis of her misery was within herself, her own belief that she was powerless to change her situation. So he could never comfort her and his first impressions were constantly reinforced until they became a concrete belief. He took this into adulthood as a belief that he could never make a woman happy. He constantly chose women, like his mother, whom he couldn't comfort. Each time he failed, he reinforced his belief in his own unworthiness. It wasn't until his third marriage broke down and he became really depressed that he sought help.

Ann was a fortunate baby, who was wanted and loved by both her parents. She absorbed this feeling of being wanted and loved from the thoughts and responses of those around her. She had the impression that she was valued and important because her parents treated her with respect. Her mother enjoyed being a woman and was confident in her sexuality. She automatically transmitted these feelings to her daughter.

Because Ann's parents handled her in a relaxed confident way, she felt secure and sensed that her parents would care for her emotional and physical needs.

Ann grew up expecting to be happy and loved because she perceived happiness and love around her. She had an innate belief that she would succeed at whatever she attempted.

When the time came for Ann to go to school, she was happy and eager to face the new experience. Because she expected everyone to like her she greeted her fellow pupils with warmth and happy smiles. And they responded to her in the same way. She reached out to them, so they liked her.

There was one child who didn't respond to her smile. He frowned and turned his back on her, then called her a name and stuck his tongue out. Now, Ann knew that she was alright, so the rudeness must be the other child's problem. She let it float over her and felt only compassion for the poor child with the problem. She certainly didn't hold it against him. Why should she? She knew that if someone has a problem, they need help. So she smiled just as warmly the next time she met him. Her warmth soon disarmed him and Ann became the only child he didn't dislike.

Because Ann believed in herself, she undertook responsibilities easily. She relaxed in class and absorbed all the lessons easily. Naturally she did well, which confirmed her belief that she would succeed.

Ann carried her beliefs into adulthood and everyone she met treated her with love and respect because she valued herself.

Because she expected to be happy, she chose to see the bright side of every situation. She chose to see the best in people and instinctively drew the best from them. She trusted people, who naturally responded to the trust she placed in them.

Her belief that people are warm, friendly and trustworthy became a reality for her, because she created it.

Life is a series of choices. Ann made daily choices to create a happy, loving environment around her. We are told that to him that hath shall be given. Ann had positive, loving, generous beliefs and to her more love and abundance were given.

Now let us look at Andy, whose beliefs and early learnings were the opposite of Ann's and so he created a very different life from hers. We are told 'From him that hath not shall be taken away' and because Andy believed he could not have what he wanted, he fulfilled those words.

Andy's mother was busy and often distracted. He had an older brother, who took a great deal of his mother's time and attention. She often couldn't feed him the moment he was hungry and his perception was that he was not important. A belief in his lack of importance was implanted in his mind.

Because he wasn't cuddled as soon as he cried, in those few moments he felt unloved. A baby is an ego-centred, feeling creature. He took in that unloved feeling as a belief he was not lovable.

Andy's mother felt slight resentment towards him because she had lost her freedom and her figure. With the demands of two small children she often felt tired and cross. She told him that of course she loved him but he was very aware of the underlying resentment. So as a small child Andy often heard her say that she loved him and yet he felt she resented him. Because of the conflicting messages, Andy became confused and anxious. He believed it was not safe to trust his intuition.

Like so many of us, Andy's parents lacked confidence, so they were over protective. Andy could sense this and felt anxious about life in general.

Whenever his parents felt angry, miserable or even despairing they still assured him that everything was alright. He sensed they were lying and his perception as a child was that he must keep his true feelings hidden. Added to this he was taught that 'big boys don't cry' and he soon learnt to repress his feelings.

Andy's parents wanted him to do well in life. Instead of encouraging him they tended to nag at him and compare him unfavourably with his older brother. He formed the impression that he could never win and started to feel hopeless.

Like so many of us Andy believed that he was unlovable and unimportant. He felt confused and anxious and unsafe. He learnt to distrust his intuition and to keep his feelings well hidden. He also perceived that however hard he tried he was not good enough to win. These beliefs were programmed into his mind and this is how he created his life.

He believed he was unlovable. This meant he expected to be rejected, so naturally he didn't reach out to people. Who reaches out when they expect to be rejected or put down? He was on the defensive. When someone made an unkind comment, he believed it and took it in and brooded over it. Therefore his belief that he was unlovable grew. This caused him to withdraw from people and build protective walls around himself.

At school he would say, 'I don't like anyone in my class', meaning 'I'm sure no one in my class could like me and I'm afraid to reach out in case I'm rejected'.

Andy watched other children playing but even if they

invited him to join them, he would shake his head. He felt too confused and unsafe. He couldn't believe they really wanted him or he feared that they would reject him later when they found out what he was really like inside. So he stayed outside the group or in the protection of one or two 'safe' friends.

As life went on Andy put up more barriers to keep people away from his vulnerable centre. He was often sarcastic, angry and rude, or critical or irritable. At other times he became quiet, withdrawn and suspicious. With some people he laughed and joked at everything, so no one got to know him or got close to him. They were all defence mechanisms which served to keep people at a distance and they all stemmed from his fear of his unworthiness.

Andy believed he could never win, so he was anxious. This meant that his mind did not absorb or retain information easily, so he found schoolwork difficult. Thus he fulfilled his beliefs and never achieved his potential.

Life presented him, too, with a series of choices and he was programmed to choose to defend and withdraw, to see hurt, to attack, to look for the worst that can happen, to mistrust.

All of us have absorbed some negative programming and we all have fears and anxieties. Our first step is to look honestly at what we have created in our lives. This enables us to see more easily what our inner beliefs are and to understand why we have needed to protect ourselves as we have done. Until we learn to change our inner beliefs, we will continue to play the negative programming in our lives, filling our lives with stress, ill health and misery. When we learn to change our beliefs for our benefit, our lives flow successfully, safely, prosperously and happily.

We are responsible for changing our own programming. We are responsible for our lives.

When we believe that we are unlovable, or unworthy or not good enough, we put barriers around ourselves to stop other people coming too close and finding out what we really feel we are like inside.

Mary was an extreme example. She was a charming, dark haired woman of thirty-five but she had never had a boy friend. She had never even been asked out on a date.

She desperately wanted a relationship and didn't know what to do. Because of her early childhood experiences, Mary had a belief that it was dangerous to let men come too emotionally close. Her mind had protected her very effectively by putting up invisible barriers to keep men away.

We worked together to remove those fears. When at an inner level she felt safe enough to let someone into her heart, a very nice man started courting her. As her inner beliefs changed, so automatically did her outer life.

The image Peter presented to the world was that of a jovial bouncy clown. Our life is a reflection of our inner beliefs, so it was clear that something different was going on at an inner level. His relationships ended in disaster. He drew self-centred shallow women, who inevitably left him. Inside he felt very hurt and angry at women.

He was in business with his father and Peter's sales always lagged behind. He felt he was letting his father down. He was prone to blinding headaches.

As a child, Peter had learnt never to show his emotions. When he felt angry or hurt, he'd cover up with the jolly clown act. His hurt and anger were expressed in headaches.

When he was a child, his mother was emotionally inconsistent. He never quite knew what to expect and so he had a belief that women caused pain and hurt. He couldn't trust them.

By the natural Law of Attraction he drew into his life what he believed. So he drew untrustworthy women who caused him pain and hurt.

Throughout his life his father had subtly discounted him, so that Peter believed he was not good enough, and could certainly never be as good as his father.

I helped him to re-educate his belief system. Learning that it was safe to acknowledge, accept and express his real feelings was a major breakthrough. By the time he'd gained in self confidence enough to stand up to his father, he didn't need to give himself headaches any more. As he believed he could be successful his sales figures rose above his father's. He saw his father as he really was, a man with faults and good points – and with that awareness came a richer, more mature relationship.

Dissolving his fears of rejection from women took longer, but as he let go of the past and learnt to trust, this attracted a new trusting relationship. Now that he has a stable relationship, a successful business and has let go of the headaches, Peter doesn't need the clown façade. He can be himself.

As his beliefs became more wholesome, he attracted wholesome relationships and situations.

Alison was a sad looking woman, who suffered from aches and pains all over her body. She had sinusitis, backache and terrible headaches. She looked far older than her true age, as if she were carrying the burdens of the world on her shoulders. From childhood she was carrying a deep feeling of being unloved and unworthy. Because of the deeply held fear that she was not lovable and not worthwhile, she repressed her anger and hurt. Inwardly she didn't feel she had the right to express those feelings.

As she realised the basis of her ill health was within her, she gradually worked to change her belief system. She learnt to value and love herself, so that others naturally valued and loved her. Over the months her tension and pain fell away.

A year after I last saw her, she wrote to say that she was in wonderful health. She felt happy and at peace because her family was close for the first time ever. She took responsibility for her life and created her own happiness and health.

FIVE

Life Choices

When my children were small we often visited Jessie, a near neighbour who had a handicapped child. Her little boy could do little more than sit and make noises. Often he screamed with rage and frustration, disrupting the household and upsetting his brother. He couldn't walk or talk. His body was unco-ordinated and yet his eyes shone with intelligence.

Jessie handled his rages with incredible patience and gentleness and responded intuitively to his needs. She knew that inside his prison he was aware but couldn't understand the language and this made his frustration so much more intense.

She and her husband decided to have another child. They really wanted a daughter and were delighted when a daughter was born to them but the little girl was also severely handicapped. Jessie's husband couldn't take it. He started to drink heavily to blot out the pain.

Throughout the years I never once heard Jessie complain. She was always accepting, as if she knew there was a purpose behind all this. With a ready smile she would help anyone.

I was the one who raged inwardly at the unfairness of life whenever I visited her.

Another neighbour was struggling to bring up her children after her husband was killed in an accident. She was short of money, had no supportive family and looked constantly pale and tired. I used to feel angry at a fate that could let this happen.

Often I talked to people burdened with debt or with illness and unable to cope with life's unequal load and I wondered why. Why is life so different for different people?

How is it that young babies hold fears and negativities? Why are some blind, some crippled and some gifted? Why do some get ill and others not?

It was not until the Laws of Karma were explained to me that everything fell into place. *Karma is the exact balance sheet of good and bad in our lives. It is the balance sheet of giving and receiving. The accounts are balanced not only day by day but over the lifetimes.*

On a daily basis, where our thoughts and deeds lie on the side of loving and giving, we earn good karma, so that happiness flows into our life.

Where the balance of our thoughts and deeds lies on the side of fear and cruelty, greed or negativity, we must repay.

And it is the same from lifetime to lifetime. We carry with us our pluses or minuses and attract good karma whenever we have earned it or problems where we have something to repay.

When we are unaware of the Spiritual Laws, we let debts mount up over the lifetimes. We think that because we got away with something, it disappears and is forgotten. I used to think in my ignorance how unfair it was that some people got away with awful things. Now I know that they are just postponing the inevitable time of repayment.

Until our soul is ready to start work we may choose easier lives. However, as we grow in awareness, at a soul level, we want to repay our debts and to put right what we have done. So a person who despoiled land in another life may be drawn to nature conservancy this time. Someone who hurt children may have an urge to look after and help children.

The Law, as we give so shall we receive, can be enforced when we come back into a new life, so what we have done to others we will have done to us. If we don't volunteer for the experience we may be persuaded by our guides and helpers that to undertake our Karma is for our higher benefit.

Perhaps someone who was a cruel, vindictive tyrant may need to experience a physical weakness or a genetic inheritance which leaves him emotionally vulnerable.

Someone who was a religious persecutor may place himself in a position where he is persecuted. Someone who misused power for personal gain may choose a position of powerlessness with a disposition which makes it difficult to assert himself.

Our lessons are karmic choices. Before we are born we have decided to attract those lessons and situations and as we learn the lessons, we are balancing our karmic accounts.

In order to have the experiences which we need for our growth during an incarnation, our Higher Self looks at all the records of our soul's progress and decides how much karma to repay, what lessons we most need to learn and how best to have the experience we need.

Then we decide on our parents, our family, our body, our sex, our nationality, our country and date of birth. Our glandular system, our genetic inheritance, family pre-dispositions, the culture we are born into are choices. The fears we need to face are pre-programmed within us.

Not a single thing happens by chance. Those difficult people and situations are there for a purpose.

One person may choose very difficult life circumstances, say poverty, cruelty, early abandonment, a weak mind, because he wants to work through a lot of karma in one life. He may choose a difficult test for his soul because he wants to learn faster.

His growth depends on how he handles those circumstances. It depends on whether he responds with bitterness and hate or with love and acceptance.

Karma can be repaid by service to others, by prayer and good thoughts, by undertaking difficult experiences with fortitude, by compassion and forgiveness. Karma can be dissolved by awareness and love.

Some people undertake karma at the beginning of their lives, some in the middle, some at the end and others all the way through.

We have all chosen in accordance with the needs of our

soul. Some of us may not be able to cope with the particular path we have chosen, but we all have the capacity to do so.

Jessie and her husband, at the level of their Higher Selves, chose to have two mentally and physically handicapped children. They moved away and I have not seen or heard of them for some years but I can look back now and surmise at the incredible lessons of acceptance and unconditional love they were learning, plus lessons of patience and great tests of faith. Probably their choice gave them many other unique lessons and tests to face which no other situation could have done. At the same time they had the opportunity to settle karmic debts.

The person who chooses a handicapped body does so to learn difficult lessons. At a higher level it is always a group family decision. Family, relations, friends, are all learning lessons with that handicapped person. So are all who come into contact with him. It is our attitude to the condition which creates our happiness and decides our growth.

When we link with someone and create karma between us, we are corded to that person until the karma is worked out and the cords dissolve.

By these cords we draw towards us people we had links with in other lives, in order that we can give or receive payment in some way. Nearly all of us are working out karmic ties with relatives and friends and we incarnate in groups again and again.

Where we have a difficult person in our lives, we are often working through a karmic relationship. In other words, we left an unresolved situation between us in another life, so we are having another try at learning to love that person unconditionally this time round.

When we feel an instant rapport or develop a rich relationship with someone, it may well be a result of good karma and we can rejoice that we have earned it.

What we do and think, how we react to people and how much we put into life, affects not only what happens to us in the near future but also what happens to us in the far future.

Many old souls are incarnating at this time, who are at the end of their karmic repayments. They have paid off all the backlog of debts in other lives and they are given the opportunity to keep the accounts up to date.

This means that if they incur more karma by negative thoughts or deeds, they pay it back at once. This is known as instant karma. If we feel we never ever get away with anything, that we are always the one who is caught, rejoice. We are receiving instant karma.

As I was writing these words in a hotel lounge, I was talking to a man, who told me this story.

When he was a boy, he threw a stick across the road for his neighbour's dog. The dog dashed after it only to be run over and killed. So this man was the instrument which caused the alsation to die.

Years later, when he started healing work, his first patient arrived. It was an alsation. The dog hated men and snarled and snapped at them, so that the young lady who owned him couldn't let a man into her life. She really wanted a boy friend.

After some months of healing sessions with the dog, he gradually became calmer and gentler and began to accept men. His owner is now a married lady with a family.

The man was able to repay the karma to the dog, if not instantly, at least within the same lifetime.

The man's story interested me for another reason. Animals' reactions are a reflection of their owners' emotions and feelings. So as he healed the dog, this man was indirectly healing the owner's unacknowledged anger towards men, enabling her to make a satisfactory relationship.

Something which is very easy for one soul to do may be very difficult for another. So we can never judge another. We do not know the amount of karma someone else has undertaken to clear. We do not know if he is a sensitive soul or a hardy soul.

A hardy holly bush may well be able to stand firm in an icy wind. We wouldn't expect a delicate hot house plant to withstand it as well? Souls are no different. There are sensitive souls and hardy souls. There are old souls and young souls. There are souls who may have had all their experiences in other planets or Universes and who may be having their first experience on the planet earth. They may feel bewildered, lost and frightened because they can't understand.

So we are in no position to criticise or condemn. We can only accept.

Our Higher Self does not choose for us to go through tests until we are ready. So what we attract, we can handle. It is when we block ourselves with fear that we find it difficult to move on. When we are open we can sense the helping hand.

Whatever happened in another life our first responsibility is to our growth in this one.

Lucy was a warm gentle woman but she had no feelings of self confidence or self worth. She had had an unsatisfactory relationship with her husband for years. He was overbearing, domineering and undemonstrative. Lucy was afraid of him and constantly allowed him to put her down. Because she was too frightened to stand up to him, she seethed with anger at him.

She told me that she had to stay with him as she was repaying karma from such and such a life when she had caused him great suffering and been very domineering to him. That may well have been true.

I felt that she was using the unpaid karma as an excuse because she was too afraid to make a break and live alone. So she stayed and suffered without trying to do anything about the situation.

If she had indeed undertaken as a karmic debt to suffer for as many years as she had made her husband suffer, she would not be able to free herself. All other pathways would be blocked until she paid her due. However she would not know until she really tried.

And as we have seen, she could also have chosen to work on herself to release her fear and anger. Then she could transmute the karma by offering him unconditional love.

So Lucy and her husband had a karmic relationship to resolve and were neither of them able to do anything about it. And instead of taking courage to free themselves from each other, they continued together in hostility and bitterness. They are busy creating a whole lot of new karma which will have to be resolved some time.

Repayment of karma is being speeded up as the planet gets ready for the leap in the growth of consciousness for which we are being prepared.

This is why many people choose to experience a number of relationships or marriages in order that they may resolve several karmic situations and clear debts.

People are attracting all sorts of difficulties and traumas into their lives to waken them up to awareness.

I have heard it said that in times of war and hardship souls queue up to be born because of the great opportunities for growth open to them.

So it may seem to our Earth eyes that the planet is in chaos and confusion, but the Divine Plan is always perfect.

SIX

Love and Fear

There are only two emotions – love and fear. Love is the acceptance of a person or situation exactly as it is – without judging, without expecting anything in return.

Anything that does not come from love comes from fear and fear is the devil we have created.

Life's lessons are to do with letting go of the old devil, fear, and replacing it with love. On the Path it helps to ask ourselves if we are ruled by love or fear. Are we ruled by God or our devil? Does our action or reaction come from love or fear?

Love is always stronger than fear. Love is light and light can always penetrate darkness. Darkness cannot put out light.

Fear is to do with the feelings of not being good enough, of not being lovable and of death or annihilation. If we are not good enough or not lovable enough, we fear we will ultimately be rejected. The rejection means we will be separate and alone.

I feel that the ultimate fear is the fear of being separate and alone. It is the fear triggered at birth by separation from the mother.

It is the fear of separation from God or the Universal energy.

It is this deepest fear which causes us to protect ourselves with walls. We shut ourselves off behind walls of fear and truly create our own separation.

The old English word hellen meant to wall off. So we create our own hell by walling ourselves off with fear.

The walls can only be dissolved from the inside by love. When we love ourselves, they automatically dissolve.

Penny held a deep fear of being abandoned. As a child she was afraid to go to school in case her mother wasn't there when she got home. Her fear became so acute that she developed a skin condition which kept her at home. The skin condition eventually became so bad that she was admitted to hospital long term, thus creating the abandonment which she so feared. She put herself into her own hell.

She married young out of fear of being alone and soon created a condition whereby her husband deserted her, re-inforcing her hell.

She is now taking responsibility for what she has created. She is learning to love herself unconditionally. As she loves herself unconditionally, she can then love others unconditionally too. This is automatically drawing love and friendships into her life.

And as she dissolves her fear with love, she is letting go of the illusion that she is separate from the Universe or God.

When she totally dissolves the fear she will never feel alone again. And she will never need to experience desertion or abandonment again. The lesson is learnt, the fear overcome. Penny will then be in tune with the Law of Love.

The Law says God is Love. As we are created by God, our essence is Love. Anything that we think, believe or do which comes from fear is naturally a contravention of the spiritual Law of Love. So where we hold onto anger, hurt, bitterness or unforgiveness, we have some work to do on ourselves to release it.

When we are jealous we fear that there is not enough love for us or that someone else is loved more. It is a belief in a limitation of love.

If our self esteem is low, it is easy to expect that parents or friends or a partner love another more. Jealous people see what they most fear in every situation.

One jealous person will so fear rejection that he will tiresomely take offence at the least thing. He will withdraw into himself, thus withdrawing love from the person who he wants to love him. This is what Terry did.

He was elderly and balding with horn rimmed glasses and he looked like everyone's idea of a genial grandfather figure. To outsiders he was outgoing and hearty but within the family it was a different story.

He took offence at the least thing, so everyone was very wary. As long as he was the centre of attention, he was happy, but if anyone withdrew attention from him, he would recede into ominous silence.

Terry was rather like a toddler demanding Mum's full attention and glowering with jealous rage when she had to deal with the other children.

His grown up children were very wary when they were with him. He would be hurt if there was any suggestion he had been left out of anything. They couldn't meet for a cup of coffee without him feeling offended. So they conspired to meet without him knowing and kept him in ignorance of family matters.

Each time he withdrew into his offended silences, Terry withdrew love from his family, the very people he wanted love from, until he excluded himself with his jealous possessiveness.

Jealousy causes another person to try to do everything possible to please and ingratiate himself with the loved one. She will lose her identity and hold on desperately and grimly until she has suffocated the other person's love.

This is what Jean did and her jealousy was equally destructive. She was pretty and birdlike, with big blue eyes, which hid a deep pool of neediness. Her first husband had left her and she had only recently re-married.

Her fear was so overpowering that she accused her new husband of fancying every female he met. She worried incessantly when he was out playing tennis with a friend. She imagined he was with another woman if he was late home from work. She even went through his pockets for tell tale signs to prove her imaginings. When she wasn't panicking and accusing him, she was clinging to him, doing everything possible to please. She lost her identity in her effort to ingratiate herself. Her poor husband never knew if he was coming home to a raging tiger or a clinging octopus.

Jean's overpowering jealous fear was too much for him and after three months he threatened to leave. At that point she sought help.

Whichever way our jealousy causes us to respond, we will create the rejection and aloneness we fear. We need to work from the inside, building up our interests, our individuality, our inner confidence.

When we feel happy about ourselves, we are whole people and we are not dependent on the approval of others. Then we can form a wholesome relationship.

Felicity had six children, all with families of their own and yet she churned with jealous rage when one of them dared to visit her brothers or sisters. Her inner insecurity was so deep she was afraid of losing a single drop of love.

She felt she was worthless and of no value without her children. They were her success, her justification for existence. Without them who was she? Who would want her? She would be alone. So she hung on grimly, making life so uncomfortable for her family that they didn't want to spend time with her and she found herself in a hell of her own creation.

People who are greedy have a deep fear that there will not be enough for them. And even if they have masses of whatever it is, they are afraid it will be taken away. There is no peace with this inner insecurity.

Anthony had resolved to move up from his poverty-stricken background to material wealth. He devoted his life to making money. And he found that now he had all that money could buy he had no inner peace. He still feared his wealth (his safety) could all be taken away from him.

Anthony felt he was valueless and vulnerable without his wealth. In the struggle for more wealth to feed his security and self esteem he had alienated all the people he cared about. If he lost his money who was he? Who would want him? He would be alone.

It was a long time before he could believe anyone could actually love him for himself.

When we feel guilty, we are tying up a lot of energy in negative thoughts. We are saying, 'I'm afraid I'm not good enough', or 'I fear I'll be judged and found wanting'. And if we aren't good enough or we're found wanting this will inevitably result in rejection.

When we feel guilty about something we've done in the past we can't undo it but we can forgive ourselves and everyone concerned. This dissolves the guilt.

Often people say, 'I simply can't forgive myself. Everyone else, yes, but myself – no.' How arrogant! How proud to think we are somehow better than everyone else.

We all make mistakes. Life is a learning experience. We would not be here if we didn't have lessons to learn. We have neither the right to judge others nor ourselves.

On earth we can only see that part of our life that we consciously know about. It is like trying to guess what the whole picture is when we hold only one or two pieces of the jigsaw in our hands.

When we review our lives at the end, we have the opportunity to see each situation in true perspective.

If we feel guilty about spending money, having nice things, being healthy or a million other things, we need to look at the underlying belief we hold about ourselves.

We deserve all that we have. Everything we possess or enjoy in our lives is drawn to us by the energy we give out or have given out in this life or another. So we have earned it and it is our right to enjoy it. By feeling guilty about the good things in our lives we are withholding thanks to God or the Universe.

If we feel guilty about not visiting a sick relative or not giving money to charity or not doing something we 'should' do, look at whose 'should' it is. Should is a parental prohibition. It is negative.

If we can't do something with openness and love it is better not to do it at all. To do anything because we feel we ought to means that we have an underlying anger when we do it and whatever good things we do will be negated by that anger. Whoever we visit because we ought to will feel that anger and be shrivelled by it.

If we still feel guilty, we need to look at the fear which

lies under our guilt. If we are inclined to feel bad about ourselves, we tend to place ourselves in no win situations so we can feel guilty whatever happens.

And when we are flagellating ourselves with guilt, we close ourselves to the Higher Powers. This means that they cannot use us for their higher purpose.

Throw guilt away. It is totally useless. Let us accept ourselves exactly as we are.

Arrogant people fear that their real self is not good enough, so they cover up with artificial arrogance. An arrogant attitude is a defence mechanism which prevents other people from getting too close. After all, if others got too close and discovered that we are really not good inside they'd reject us and we'd be alone.

Sarcasm, nastiness, rudeness, flippancy, shyness, constant talking, all serve the underlying purpose of keeping people at a distance. They say, 'I don't feel safe inside. I'm afraid you'll find I'm not good enough and you'll reject me', so keep away.

A ten year old girl said to me one day that she hated every single child in her class. She had told me about various of her classmates, so I asked if she'd like Rod if he liked her. She said she would. Yes and she'd like Mary if Mary liked her. Suddenly she said eagerly 'I'd like them all if they'd like me first'.

How many of us do this under the guise of shyness or lack of confidence? We stay in hell behind our walls and wait for someone to reach out to us first.

I was in a supermarket one day when I very timid lady said, 'Excuse me, would you mind if I stretch across you for some oranges'. I said, 'Of course', and made room for her. She told me that someone had just been very nasty to her when she'd tried to reach for something.

I said that sometimes people got very uptight and it was a good idea just to send them some love if they had none to give. She blinked a little thoughtfully.

Later she stopped me and said, 'Thank you for pointing that out to me. It helped me to see it all differently'.

If someone is too tired to give you a smile, give them one instead. When we find ourselves using controls and manipulations, we need to look at the fear we have of what will happen if we let go.

Most children learn to manipulate and control their parents from an early age. They can't assume direct power, so they find more subtle ways of getting attention or their own way.

Mothers are often heavily into controlling and manipulating husbands and children – especially if motherhood is their justification for existence. Nor are men strangers to subtle use of pressure.

Here are just a few common ways of manipulating others:

    sulking, bad moods, huffiness
    being late, being slow, being early
    refusing to eat, fussy eaters
    being unpredictable, being easily hurt, tears
    being angry, being depressed, being tired
    money, bribes, threats
    illness, headaches, backaches

These manipulations are the survival strategies we learn to get our needs met as children and they are the very things we need to pinpoint to release.

Whoever grabs the TV remote control in your family is in control of the viewing choices. They are grabbing power.

One person I know is like a big black spider, controlling everyone with the unspoken threat she'll go into a black mood and spoil the whole day if the family is not nice to her. And the family colludes with her manipulation by being nice to her, and they all seethe underneath.

Frederick was a high powered businessman. He was always unwell at weekends. On Monday mornings he would get up, alive, excited and ready to work, only to be ill the following weekend. And of course the illness was genuine.

As a child he'd learnt that illness was the best way to get attention and it soon became clear to him as an adult that the family didn't notice him when he was well. They fussed over him when he was ill. So Dad, quite unaware of what he was doing, controlled the weekend with illness.

Backaches, headaches, all types of illness can unconsciously be used as manipulating and controlling mechanisms. Like all survival strategies, they served a purpose at one time, but sometimes they continue long after their purpose is served.

Boredom is a wonderful way of blotting out something we don't want to see or hear. If we get bored with our friendships or relationships, maybe we are afraid of someone coming any closer. Boredom puts the shutters up and defends us from intimacy. If we fear failure we can become bored in class or with a job. It becomes a justification for failing. 'It's no wonder we didn't do well', we say, 'It was so boring'. Loneliness too says I'm afraid of people coming too close to me. I'd rather be lonely than risk hurt or rejection.

June came to me in distress. She had to spend Christmas at her in-laws and her mother-in-law hated her and did hurtful things to her. It was so awful that June didn't know how she could cope.

We looked at the fears June's mother-in-law held and why she needed to treat June as she did.

Instantly June saw her mother-in-law differently. She realised that the jealousy, the sarcasm, the rejections, the put downs were her mother-in-law's problems. June went to stay with them at Christmas with a new attitude – open and excited to see what she could learn. With her new awareness, she smiled at what she now recognised as her mother-in-law's problems and let the comments float over her.

On one occasion when her mother-in-law ignored her and gave the entire family a second helping and 'forgot' her, June felt her stomach contract in anger. But instead of getting hooked into the old familiar feelings of impotent rage, she let the awareness come up that this too was her mother-in-law's problem. June knew that she could choose whether or not to be hurt or to return love.

She relaxed and breathed deeply, repeating to herself,

'This is her problem. I am perfect as I am,' and the pain in her tummy went.

She chose to respond with love and not fear. Because June was not responding with the usual anger and walls and daggers, her mother-in-law began to feel safe and started to warm towards her.

By the end of the holiday, June knew that the relationship with her mother-in-law had changed.

Love has a magic quality of healing.

Without fear we are love. Love energises and brings to life. Love can never be drained because the supply is limitless, as its source is the Universal energy. Love gives freely and unstintingly and always comes back to us in some way.

SEVEN

The Law of Cause and Effect

A single thought sends out an energy. Several people transmitting the same thought multiplies that energy. That force can exert a powerful influence on people or events.

When a number of people hold the same belief they radiate that belief with such strength that others unconsciously pick it up and absorb it.

Families commonly hold a collective belief, for example, 'We Smiths are always unlucky'. The whole family is sending out a negative expectation, creating and attracting its own misfortune.

I've heard, 'We all sleep badly in our family'. Bad sleep patterns aren't hereditary. However, the collective expectation of bad sleep is a potent force which can create havoc with the sleep patterns of the family.

Collective thoughts and beliefs can of course be powerfully positive.

'We're a friendly bunch in our house,' is a wonderful feeling to transmit. Everyone's friendliness rubs off onto everyone else's, filling the home with a welcoming atmosphere, which everyone absorbs and enjoys.

Most of us have experienced going into an empty house and feeling relaxed in the peaceful atmosphere. Yet in another house there has been a sense of gloom. We are picking up the thought vibrations left by the people who have been living there and we are affected by them during our visit. For sensitive people it can be totally destructive to live continuously in a bad atmosphere.

Families create their own energy and it influences them and other people.

All matter absorbs, holds and radiates energy. *When we fill our homes with love and laughter, the very fabric absorbs that joyous energy and radiates it for all to share.*

Each individual can do his bit. A family can create a home which is a positive beacon of light into the world.

When we fill our homes with joy and peace and happiness, we do more good than we realise. Even passers-by can be touched by the positive energy.

Communities hold collective beliefs. A commonly held limiting belief in our community is that old people become ill or dependent or lonely – even useless. This means that as people become older they respond to that expectation. Indeed, there is some wear and tear on the body but most of the illness, the useless feeling and the sense of isolation are created in the mind.

It's a good idea to start telling ourselves now that we're going to be happy, healthy and surrounded by love to the end of our days!

In fact many communities hold beliefs that the old people amongst them are venerable, respected, integrated and healthy – and so they become.

If a family allows a situation to develop where father is authoritarian and domineering and where the children are expected to be unquestioningly obedient, then that family is creating a dictator as father. When there are enough families dominated by a dictator, that community will create a dictator as its leader.

If on the other hand enough families develop honest communication, fairness, a sense of justice and equality with all its members, then a government will be created which reflects these qualities.

Collective beliefs are naturally more powerful than individually held beliefs.

If a team believes it is the best, it is invincible.

If enough people hold angry, violent thoughts, the result will be war.

If enough people hold peace and love in their thoughts there must be peace.

When we think negative, angry, fearful thoughts and

energise them by brooding, we give that black cloud of thoughts a life of its own. It then floats away and joins other dark energy clouds.

When we watch films where cruelty and war and murder are shown, a great anger is aroused. If we churn over the feelings of impotence and rage and vengeance, we release that energy into the ether. Imagine it multiplied by hundreds of thousands of viewers all sending out anger. That negativity forms a free floating dark energy cloud. This can attach to receptive individuals and create havoc.

Perhaps a brooding loner picks it up and becomes a killer, or a gang of teenagers is open to it and become rowdy, or a restless crowd becomes violent.

The most powerful way of activating the inner mind is by showing it a picture. If you imagine you have a slice of sharp juicy lemon in your mouth, you may be able to evoke the taste and smell. Then you will probably find you have extra saliva in your mouth or that you want to swallow.

If you do have a physical response, it is because you showed your mind a picture of a lemon. Your computer examined its memory banks for a response and gave you a physical feed back. You are responding to the suggestion made by the picture.

People with allergic asthma wheeze at the sight of plastic flowers. Dare to talk about head lice and watch how many people scratch their scalps. If a lecturer keeps clearing his throat, notice how many people in the audience follow suit.

We are all suggestible. Television is a powerful influence because it constantly presents us with pictures to which we respond. Unconsciously we accept the instructions and suggestions contained in the pictures.

When a smoker sees someone smoking on television, his inner mind is responding by creating a physical response to a cigarette. Naturally he then starts to crave one.

If we are drinkers and we see someone pouring out a

drink, talking about it and savouring it, automatically our recorded responses to alcohol are activated. We begin to crave a drink.

If we watch a violent film, a seed of violence is stirred within us.

Naturally, heroism, devotion, caring, beauty and all positive qualities can also be activated within us.

A TV film showing rape may stir up a deep rooted sexual violence within us of which we are unaware because we've always repressed the thoughts. Multiply this feeling by a million viewers and an energy blast of sexual violence forms and lurks in the Universe, like a dark cloud. If this attaches to a sexually frustated person, he may become a rapist.

Not one of us is totally pure. We wouldn't be on earth if we were. We would be on a higher plane. So we all have negativities.

We all generate negative thoughts which contribute to mass violence or disasters. So we are all collectively responsible.

As a nation we exercise a collective choice about what is presented on our TV programmes. What we are given is a response to what we want or believe we deserve.

At the moment we are choosing violence and negativity, with its inevitable boomerang effect of more violence and low quality expectations about life and we are all collectively contributing to this.

Look at the positive side. A film is shown on starvation in Ethiopia. A million people are touched with compassion and it forms an energy cloud which is picked up by Bob Geldof, who is inspired and energised to form Live Aid and Band Aid. That energy of compassion worked like a dynamo, triggering generosity in the hearts of millions.

As each individual takes responsibility for raising his thoughts, the consciousness of the nation will automatically raise.

Then our TV programmes will reflect this, beaming education, peace and happiness to us. Films will be inspirational, news items of heroism and joy.

People will no longer go to bed after watching morbid, depressing news, or a violent film, tense with fear and unable to sleep.

How pleasant when we can choose to end the day with a relaxing, peaceful film, so that we can all enjoy healing, relaxing sleep and dreams.

So called disasters are man made. Vast cumulative clouds of negative energy fasten on to the earth to create earthquakes where there is a weakness.

Enough blazing anger creates fires. Enough sexual fear creates sexually transmitted diseases. Floods and hurricanes are created by the emotional energy we release. Sometimes these take place where no one is living. This is the referred pain effect which happens in the body of the Earth as it does in the body of man.

We do not live in a haphazard Universe. All matter is subject to the Law of Cause and Effect.

We are individually and collectively masters of our destiny. We are not only responsible for our lives. We are also responsible for our world.

Thoughts are a powerful energy. They can be sent to heal people, to pacify situations and to heal the earth.

When we sit back and say there is nothing we can do about a situation, we are abrogating responsibility.

We can, each and every one, send healing, loving thoughts to every person in need, every situation of pain or anger or any place where there is unhappiness.

Sense the black cloud emanating from prisons. Sense the black cloud coming from slaughterhouses and battery farms. Sense the pain round a hospital. Where there is an individual or a place crying out in pain and fear we can send in our golden compassion and healing thoughts.

Each positive thought we send will join the golden clouds of energy and create magical effects on the world and on ourselves.

We can each of us contribute to changing the world for good by the positive, wholesome, generous, healing thoughts we radiate.

As we each of us become more aware of our power to dissipate the negativity both within us and in the collec-

tive, the move to peace and joy must speed up.
We can each play a part.

EIGHT

Anger

Many people are confused by anger. Is it always bad? Does it serve any constructive purpose?

In order to protect our young, to right injustices or to defend ourselves, we need a positive charge of energy.

Our bodies were designed so that if we met danger in the jungle, a boost of adrenalin would give us the impetus to run away or to fight. When we'd run clear of the danger or used the energy fighting it, the adrenalin was used up and the body and mind returned to peace and tranquillity.

And of course, if you see a person or animal being mistreated, it is appropriate to use a positive charge of energy to rescue it. This is a clear, red energy, which dissolves as soon as action is taken.

A baby uses anger energy to make sure it gets necessary food and attention. You are in no doubt when a baby is angry. It really wants soemthing, and when its need is satisfied, peace returns.

However, if, instead of using the energy for appropriate action, we churn it round inside us, it becomes a murky dark red. This is what I mean by anger.

So if the baby does not get his needs met the energy impulse becomes dark anger. This is because black fear that he cannot get his needs met is mixing with the anger energy.

A toddler who cannot get the attention, love and understanding he wants will naturally shout or have a tantrum. He has no other way of asking for what he wants.

And if the youngster is chastised or banished to his

room when he gets angry, he soon learns to hide those murky dark red feelings.

He has to learn to survive within the rules of that particular family and so repressing angry feelings is for him the only way to survive. Repression becomes a survival mechanism.

Chastisement and banishment are obvious punishments. More subtly, parents use hurt looks, a slight coolness, a tightening of the lips, so that the child picks up a feeling that it is bad to be angry.

Vaguely worded threats are a powerful controlling mechanism to keep a child in line. The ways people in authority bring pressure to bear on sensitive children to repress their feelings are limitless – and as a mother I'm sure I've tried them all.

When pressure is brought onto a child to deny his anger, he will swallow it down. If swallowed it goes inside and can turn to sore throats, tummy aches or ear aches. A lifetime of suppression can lead to depression or cancer or arthritis or any other illness.

A child may try to get its own back by stealing or cheating or bullying.

Very commonly little girls turn their anger into tears because it is more acceptable in our society for girls to cry than to be angry. Many women cry when anger would be a more appropriate response.

Because they have had to suppress their anger for so long, many people do not think they have any. They have been 'nice' for so many years that they are often totally unaware of their real feelings.

It is hardly surprising. After all, if our very survival depends on hiding our feelings and being nice, we pretty soon believe we are the niceness we pretend. To believe anything else would be death.

Many people suspect that anger is a raging tiger within them and are terrified of what it would do if unleashed.

Some use alcohol to depress their inhibitions. I've heard people say, 'He only gets violent when he's drunk'. It sounds like an excuse. In fact, it means that when that person drinks, it is the only time he can get in touch with the unexpressed pent up rage inside him.

He uses drink to give himself permission to release the lid on the volcano within.

Lots of people deflect their anger, like the man who is furious with his wife and takes his rage out behind the wheel. The resulting accident is his expression of his feelings.

The child who is upset at school and comes out of the school gates and kicks Mum, is deflecting feelings. So is the woman who feels angry with the children and takes it out on the dog or her husband.

The toddler who is angry at the attention the new baby is getting has to 'love' the baby to please Mummy. She has to behave like a good girl to keep Mummy loving her, so she puts her feelings down and wets the bed or has nightmares.

Many a woman is chained, emotionally or physically, to parents or family and lets herself be put down or manipulated. Often a woman like this comes to me with her whole physical body screaming in protest. She may even be paralysed with rage. Generally she smiles sweetly as she denies all anger or frustration.

She almost certainly feels she has no rights – and she probably gave them away at an early age. She may need to accept her right to be angry before she can acknowledge the anger.

Then she can look at and release the fear underlying the anger.

When we churn anger over in our minds we 'hold' that tension in part of our body. Extra blood churns around the body in response to the angry thoughts and of course it can't flow through easily where the body is in tension. So we start creating physical problems in our bodies at that point. We create a block there.

Anger uses up a great deal of energy. When we use a second charge of energy to suppress the anger, we are tying up a high proportion of our available energy. If we suppress anger for long enough it uses all our energy and leads to depression.

Suppressing anger creates an energy block in our body

which devitalises and exhausts us. It drains the life force.

Anger shows in our auras as a murky red blob and attracts towards us a person with a similar murky red blob. Then we rub off angrily on each other. We irritate each other. There is an atmosphere between us.

Everyone we draw into our lives is there for a purpose. Each is a mirror of some aspect of ourselves – positive or negative. When someone makes us angry, irritates us, upsets us, hurts us, they are there for a purpose. They are showing us that there is something within us that we need to look at.

No one can arouse anger or hurt or frustration or irritation unless it is within us to trigger.

That murky red blob of energy in our aura can attract situations into our lives.

Accidents, fires, scaldings, explosions are drawn to us by our anger. Because I believe that nothing happens by chance, it follows that there is no such thing as an accident or an Act of God.

People used to think that disasters were punishments by the gods for their sins. In fact the disasters were the natural boomerang effect of the collective negativity that was being emitted, absorbed by nature and returned.

Because everything we draw into our lives is attracted to something we are sending out, each happening is telling us about our innermost thoughts and giving us an opportunity to learn.

Whatever we are feeling or thinking at a deep, unaware level, the Universe will give to us in order that we may question and grow. When people scald or burn themselves or someone else, look for what they were seething with rage about.

Years ago I tipped a pressure cooker of steaming soup down my leg. I was seething about the situation I was in in my life. In those days I was a victim of life and I thought, 'Poor me; now look what's happened to me'.

In fact my inner processes were showing me that I was very angry about my situation and it was time I took responsibility and did something about it.

The wife who scratches her husband's new car is taking

her irritation out on him in the only way she can, without realising it. Many a 'nice' person does this. They often deny their anger and do not want to take responsibility for it.

One client who had come to recognise that his whole family was seething with anger towards him, though they never dared to express it openly, told me that his wife and teenage children had had several accidents while driving his car and none when driving their own! It was their only way of venting their rage at him.

If the whole household is blazing mad, it can manifest as a house fire. If the whole community is aflame with rage, the whole area can go up in flames.

Violence is an obvious manifestation of anger, but what about the 'innocent' victim?

One person may deeply fear violence, and it can be a fear of which they are not conscious. They then draw violence to themselves. Someone else may be very nice and spiritual on the surface and be a seething mass of murderous feelings inside, thus drawing the violent energy that they are unknowingly sending out.

We are often not consciously aware of our deepest feelings and it is only when we attract a trauma into our lives that we have the opportunity to recognise them and work to release them.

All traumas contain the gift of a lesson. At an ego level they are painful to deal with and need understanding and compassion and healing. At a higher level we attract traumas to learn.

What may be a pinprick to one soul may be a deep, deep, hurtful trauma for another. It may be something uncleared over many lives and the lessons, and therefore the traumas, get more and more difficult until we are forced to face them.

Some people believe that the only way to get out anger is to beat it out into a cushion – in other words to get in touch with the feelings and express them. If in doubt get it out.

If you do repress your feelings or indeed if you've kept them in so long that you no longer experience feelings, it can help enormously to acknowledge, experience and release the trapped energy physically, by shouting and screaming it out.

Be aware that you are letting go of a dark red energy from within you to outside. Once outside it will create personal havoc for you or will join the cumulative dark cloud of anger in the Universe, unless transmuted into light.

So when we do express anger and release negative energy blocks from within, a healing ceremony should be performed to clear the air.

We can do this by imagining gold flowing from our hearts and dissolving the dark cloud – or we can fill the room with golden thoughts. Then visualise the situation or person in question and forgive them and send them love. We need to forgive ourselves too.

The release of emotion, together with the healing and forgiveness, will bring an understanding of the situation from the other person's point of view. The shift in perception allows a healing to take place within us.

I do not believe that it is necessary to release and express anger by screaming and shouting in order for a physical release to take place within.

When someone or something makes us feel tense or angry we can say thank you for drawing our awareness to the block within us. As we acknowledge our anger and accept it, we are able to look within at the underlying fear.

Dissolving the underlying fear with wisdom and love releases the energy block, physically as well as emotionally.

NINE

Creating Our Reality

How we perceive the world depends on the beliefs we hold.

We see what we expect to see.

We hear what we expect to hear.

We can do what we believe we can do.

We allow ourselves to have what we believe we deserve.

If the truth is one thing and we see only the parts that we expect to see, our reality about that truth is subjective.

Because the energy of the Universe automatically gives each of us what we expect and believe we deserve, we each create our own subjective reality.

When we believe something, we expect it to happen and expectation is much stronger than desire. So we get what we expect to happen not what we want to happen.

We all see what we expect to see. Pauline did not believe deep down that she was beautiful or good enough. Her husband was a very charming and attractive man and loved her very much. He was outgoing and gregarious and liked people. When they went to a firm dinner dance he danced several times with Pauline and he danced with and talked to most of the other wives. He was astonished when Pauline accused him of ignoring her and dancing with one of his colleague's beautiful young wives. It led to a row.

When Pauline discussed her distress with me, we looked at the true reality. Most of the wives were elderly and her husband had danced with each one. He had also danced once with the beautiful young wife of his colleague. Pauline too had been dancing and socialising most of the evening.

When her husband danced with the elderly wives, she hadn't registered it, but she selectively saw that he danced only with the young beautiful one.

Because of her fears she saw what she expected to see and ignored everything else.

As she became more aware she noticed that she often selectively saw when her husband talked to attractive women. It was only when her own inner security became stronger and she began to feel more attractive and confident inside that she was able to see objectively.

When I was getting divorced I painted some pictures. My father visited the house on several occasions while I was painting and made a number of comments about the pictures.

He did not want to accept that I was leaving my husband and closed his eyes and ears to all that I said and did. When I moved, I hung the paintings in the sitting room of my new home. They were there for four years.

I decided to marry again and my father's fears about me relaxed. To my astonishment he asked when and where I'd bought the new pictures. It was safe for him to see and hear things about me again. Until that moment he neither saw the pictures nor remembered our conversations.

We hear what we choose to hear. We can all selectively hear our name mentioned in a crowded room. Exhausted mothers sleep through overhead thunderstorms but hear their babies cry.

One woman believes all men are untrustworthy. She wants to trust the men in her life but she expects them to let her down. She acts on the defensive, warily, suspiciously, without being aware of it and her expectations are answered.

So men really are untrustworthy with her. This confirms the belief, so she is justified in believing that men are untrustworthy, for it is the personal reality she has created.

Another believes all men are dependable and trustworthy. Her father was. Her brothers were. She trusts men openly and freely. The men in her life respond. They wouldn't dream of letting her down and they fulfil her belief. Her reality is that men are trustworthy.

These two women live in the same world, subject to the same Laws and the Law says we will be given what we believe. Everyone knows the secret beliefs held in those women's hearts by what happens to them.

One person believes he will always get a car parking space. Another believes he can never park in town. The Universe responds by making a space available for the first and not for the second. Their reality is truly different.

We allow ourselves to have what we believe we deserve.

Sonia had a very low sense of worth. She wore hand me down clothes. She never had enough money. She moved from awful accommodation to worse and she didn't think she deserved anything better.

We talked for some time about her lifestyle and expectations and I suggested that perhaps it was time to let herself have the best. She agreed that she did deserve the best.

She had to move house and looked at two apartments. One was beautiful and luxurious, the other dirty and dingy.

Because of her belief in her unworthiness, she actually accepted the dirty, dingy one and drove home feeling depressed and cross with herself.

Over a cup of coffee, she thought about deserving the best. Shouting aloud, 'I deserve the best. I deserve the best', she ran to the telephone to accept the lovely apartment and to turn the dingy one down.

Sonia was full of joy as she moved into the beautiful apartment. For two weeks she felt wonderful, until the underlying belief in her unworthiness surfaced. Then she created a situation whereby she lost the beautiful home and found herself back in dingy accommodation again, which is what she really felt she deserved.

Because of her underlying belief, she had only allowed herself to have the best for two weeks. She was extremely aware and knew exactly what she'd done and how she had created what happened. She decided that her self worth was so low that it was a very positive move forward that she had allowed herself to have the best for two weeks and that she must build on that for the future.

The energy of expectation is stronger than that of desire, which is why we get what we inwardly expect to happen and not what we want to happen.

Spiritual Law tells us that the secret desires of our heart will be answered and this means, the unexpressed inner beliefs we hold will be answered. Thus we create our own subjective reality for the Truth is that the Universe is perfect.

Imagine a crystal clear lake. Every pebble on the bottom is clearly visible, every fish bright and colourful. It is a wonderland of beauty.

On the surface float glass bottomed boats. One man has painted the glass bottom of his boat black. Because he can see nothing, he believes there is nothing there to see. His reality is blackness.

Another has allowed the bottom of his boat to become filthy. He scoffs at the stories of beauty. Through the dirt he sees the beautiful fish as lurking monsters. He fears the lake is full of danger.

A third man's boat has a glass bottom which is streaky and cloudy. He has occasional flashes of clarity and is vaguely aware of 'something' but it seems dull and distorted.

And yet another keeps the glass clear and polished, working ceaselessly to this end. He knows the beauty is there. To him it is clear and obvious. He will try to describe the wonderful world he sees to others. They may scoff or be incredulous. Or they may decide to clean up the glass screens on their boats in the hope that they will see what he sees.

When we are told that the lake is clear and beautiful and that the dirt and lurking monsters are within our imagination, it is an act of faith to clear away the dirt.

Yet even the person with the most deeply ingrained dirt to clear can do it.

The more diligently and enthusiastically we dedicate

ourselves to clearing up the dirt within us, the more help we receive in our task and the more quickly we see the light.

Because our mind holds our belief system about ourselves and about life itself, we see what we expect to see. We see outside us what lies within us.

If we believe the world is full of fearful lurking monsters and is an unsafe place, it is time to start a clear out.

The reality of the lake was that it was crystal clear and beautiful. Each person saw it through a different screen and therefore saw it differently.

The reality of the Universe is that it is love and light. Anything that we perceive that is not love and light is within ourselves.

This is why, when we hate someone, whatever we hate about them is an unacknowledged lurking monster, within us.

If someone cheats and we feel tense with fury, then we need to look at the unacknowledged part of us that wants to cheat. If it were not within us, we would accept the person calmly exactly as he is, without condemning him for cheating. Cheating is our lurking monster and the person we hate is offering us a chance to learn about ourselves.

I used to be very judgemental and critical but as I've acknowledged and accepted so many of those lurking monsters I had locked away, I'm much more accepting and grateful to people for the lessons they offer me. I've a great many more lessons to learn. In fact the more I acknowledge about my shadow side, the more I find there is to look at.

Every single time we face a monster, with courage, we are rewarded.

Gwen had gone through a relationship with a married man who was an alcoholic and a liar. She felt she'd learnt a great many lessons about valuing herself. For her next relationship, she drew in a very attractive man, a heavy drinker who messed her about by being unrealiable. After a few dates she learnt he was married. She found him fun and good company and wanted to hold on to the relationship. She also wanted someone in her life, rather than no-one.

We looked at what was happening and she reluctantly admitted to herself that she was being tested. She took a positive decision and telephoned him to cancel her date for the next evening and tell him that she didn't want to see him again.

The phone immediately rang with a supper invitation for the next evening. At that supper she met a wholesome man with whom she had a great deal in common, a man who valued her and treated her with respect.

She chose to be strong and was rewarded. If she had stayed with weakness and gone out with the married man, she wouldn't have met the right man for her.

Every day of our lives we make choices, big and small, which affect our lives and the lives of those around us.

> To wallow or to make a new life with courage.
> To think bad of another or look for the good.
> To think depressed or happy thoughts.
> To hate or to forgive wholeheartedly.
> To find fault or praise.
> To stay stuck or make decisions and implement them.
> To give up or to fight.
> To be a victim or in charge of life.
> To blame others or to accept self-responsibility.

Polly hated her mother-in-law. The old lady was in an expensive nursing home, which was eating into the family finances. Polly's husband paid his mother's expenses and gave her gifts which deprived the family. Polly's rage was enormous and she couldn't find a single good word to say about the demanding, greedy, querulous old lady.

When we examined the reality of the situation, Polly acknowledged her jealousy and saw that her mother-in-law was just a sad lonely old woman, who wanted to be loved and was terrified of being abandoned and alone. She was filled with an unexpected compassion. That afternoon Polly visited her mother-in-law for the first time in some weeks and actually saw her in a new light.

The next day the old lady died peacefully in her sleep. Polly had learnt her lesson and the old lady was freed. So was the money she had been costing.

When Polly chose to look for the good instead of seeing the bad, she was rewarded.

Helen had had many rejections in her life and she chose to see hurt and rejection in every situation. She moved to the sixth form of a new College and felt that all the teachers hated her, as indeed she felt they had done at her last school. One in particular, whom she called Miss Piggy, picked on her and would never give her a chance to show her acting talent.

I tried gently to help her see the problem was within herself, but she chose to remain a victim, wallowing in hurt and blame.

I saw her a week later and she told me that she'd gone home and thought maybe her attitude was just a little responsible for what happened so she'd decided to change it.

'You won't believe this,' she said. I smiled. 'Miss Piggy actually smiled at me . . . smiled, Miss Piggy! Then she asked me to audition for a part in the school play. It's unbelievable.'

Within a few days of choosing to change herself, there was an answering response.

Bruce had had a quarrel with his father many years ago. He saw his mother secretly but harboured resentment towards his father. His marriage had broken down and he was full of anxiety. He was in debt and smoking enormously. Both his health and his bank balance were badly damaged.

He had sought help everywhere for his smoking problem but nothing seemed to help his addiction. I felt he couldn't let go of the smoking until he forgave his father. He agreed with me.

He took his courage in his hands and went to see his father and they healed the relationship. Within a few weeks he met a rich widow who loved him as he was. He was rewarded for choosing to forgive his father. He was loved and financially secure. He came back to me for a single session to work on his smoking problem and gave it up easily.

His forgiving attitude brought him health, love and prosperity.

Look for the Divine in every man and the Divine responds.

TEN

The Inner Child

All the events of our lives are stored away on a kind of microfilm in our minds.

People constantly trigger emotions within us. Those same emotions were originally experienced by the small child and stored as feelings. The original feeling of the experience is then locked into the inner computer at that age.

A sentence, an experience, a person, a smell can trigger something within us and that trigger activates the mind to search its memory banks for the emotional response it has stored away.

This is why people become inexplicably and inappropriately hurt or angry or fearful at something seemingly trivial. *Over the top responses and reactions always mean that an uncleared feeling at the level of the inner child has been activated.*

Jim was a middle aged man with everything money could buy but he had no inner peace. He brooded over everything and ruled his family and his work force with anger. Everyone was afraid of his rages.

He told me that his brother was born when he was seven years old. Jim felt shut out and unloved. He felt no one wanted him any more. He ran away but when he returned he was sent to his room and this reinforced his feeling of being unloved.

I asked him to shut his eyes and go back to the time when his brother was born and see himself then.

He saw himself as a seven year old lying on the floor kicking and screaming, having a terrible tantrum.

I told him to bring his mother into his inner scene. He

said that she looked angry with him, so I suggested he put his arms round her and tell her that he loved her.

This time he said that she looked puzzled. 'Put your arms around her again,' I coaxed, 'And tell her that you love her'.

He agreed to try. 'Oh!' he exclaimed. 'She's crying – and she says she loves me but she's so tired she can't cope.' His face beamed. 'She really does love me.'

He saw himself and his mother walk hand in hand to a stream and wash away all the hurt and pain in the pure water. He kept holding her hand tightly and laughing.

When he opened his eyes he exclaimed. 'She really loved me. And all my life I thought she didn't care.'

Throughout Jim's life, whenever he felt or perceived a rejection, he had responded as the hurt seven year old, with anger. All hurts and rejections triggered that original terrible feeling within him.

Now that the memory in his mind was healed, he no longer needed to respond with anger. He changed and everyone responded quickly.

His children started to bring their friends home for the first time ever. His wife phoned me to say they were happy at last in their marriage. Productivity at work increased as he relaxed with his work force.

And Jim started to allow himself to love and be loved.

It is important to remember that we store memories as we perceived the situation at that time and not as it actually occurred.

So the two year old may observe his parents having a quarrel which soon passes over. But the imprint he stores in his mind is his perception of what happened. And at a two year old level he may perceive his parents as two giants engaged in a life and death struggle where he feels like a small helpless being about to be annihilated.

He may go into inner shock and until that memory is healed or new learnings take its place, he may go into shock whenever he is in the presence of a quarrel.

Many people cannot handle anger in others because it triggers their childhood feelings of impotence and terror.

A happily married lady with a young family came to me because she couldn't control her weight. She always wanted to nibble.

The core of her problem was that her father had died when she was a child. From that time she had felt insecure, unloved and guilty, so she compensated by nibbling.

I asked her to relax deep inside herself and imagine herself just before her father died. A terrible feeling of emptiness and loneliness welled up inside her.

She watched her parents come into her inner scene and she cried out in anguish and disbelief as her mother turned away from her. The little girl was devastated. It took time for the child to understand that her mother had not in reality turned away from her but that she had perceived her mother's grief reaction as such. When she accepted this, she relaxed again and felt safe inside.

She could easily see and feel herself cuddle up to her father but the little child could not understand why he'd left her. Nor was she able to forgive him for abandoning her by dying.

Forgiveness is an essential part of the healing process and she wanted to complete the healing.

The Universe gave her the opportunity to explore her feelings more deeply. That very week, more than thirty years after his death, there was a reunion of all her father's friends at an exhibition of his life's work. He was brought constantly to her awareness.

In the next session she relaxed easily and saw herself again as a child.

Her mother was cross and every time she asked for a cuddle she was pushed away. The small child sobbed, 'Nobody loves me'.

I explained to the child that her mother loved her very much but was so blocked off with grief that she couldn't reach out to her. Gradually the child understood and was able to reach out to her mother. The child forgave her mother and the two of them held each other close. Suddenly the child laughed with sheer joy.

One part of the healing was complete.

We asked her Daddy to come into the scene and she ran over to him at once.

He talked gently to her and helped her to understand how truly deeply he loved her. He told her of his sorrow that he had to leave her.

'Oh that feels much better inside,' she breathed. She clung onto him as if she never wanted to let him go. Then she really forgave him for leaving her. We both felt his presence very strongly in the room. Whenever I saw her after that she referred to that magic moment of healing and how different she felt inside.

Janet's mother died when she was quite small. Two older siblings died in babyhood before Janet was born.

I asked her to see herself as a child and she saw and felt the desolation of the child whose mother had died.

Her adult self went into her inner scene and gave the child Janet all the cuddling and cradling she craved at that moment. She promised the child she'd always care for her and look after her. And when the child felt safe and trusting she took her into her heart.

Then Janet suddenly went deep into trance and appeared distressed. She wouldn't talk to me so I brought her out of trance and asked her to open her eyes.

She told me that she'd suddenly experienced an awful feeling. She saw herself as a child, crying. Two children who were with her were being dragged away and she had to go somewhere else alone.

We realised at once that these were the two siblings who had died. She had to leave them and be born alone. She was very happy then to visualise herself releasing them with love.

When she'd done this she saw herself run and wash in a waterfall. Then she danced in the sunlight to symbolise that she was free to be herself without the unseen influence of her unknown siblings.

When she opened her eyes she said she felt freed of a burden that she'd always carried without realising it.

At the next session she was ready to heal the inner child who felt abandoned by her mother. When the healing was complete, the child was able to wave goodbye quite happily and calmly to her mother.

It always gives me an incredible feeling inside when someone lets go of a loved one with joy.

When we experience a feeling as a child we constantly try to recreate that feeling throughout our lives. It does not matter how awful the feeling is. We will somehow put ourselves into situations again and again when we have the same feeling. The circumstances may seem different each time but the feeling remains the same.

This will continue until we decide to look at what we are creating and do something about it. When we have a belief or fear, the Universe will give us opportunity after opportunity to experience it until we decide to release it. Thus we evolve by releasing our fears.

Paulette was thirty five but her wide grey eyes held such a vulnerable expression that she looked much younger. As a child she'd always felt left out and abandoned. In adulthood it would somehow transpire that she was left out in small ways. And when her husband left her she was truly abandoned.

She was full of rage and constantly experienced the fear of being abandoned.

So she agreed to close her eyes and seek the child part of herself she had had to abandon. She found herself going down into a cellar and there she was, five years old, completely naked, neglected, dirty, thin and hungry, chained to a wall.

She explained to the child that she had come to free her. When she had cut the chains she asked the child what she needed first.

'My Mummy.'

So Paulette told her that she was here to look after the child. She promised that she would always be there for the child and would never leave her again. The child relaxed then as Paulette freed her and wrapped her in a blanket.

Carefully covering her eyes, she carried the child into the light. She took her to a little cottage nearby and bathed her gently all over, including her hair, to cleanse her

symbolically. Then she wrapped her in a huge soft towel
and took her into the kitchen for food and drink. Thus she
symbolically nourished her.

In the bedroom she found laid out a little white dress –
new beginnings. When she carried the frail child out into
the garden, she still had her eyes closed.

Paulette introduced the little girl to the feel of a warm
pebble in her hand, to the touch of grass under her feet, to
the perfume of a flower and the sound of a bird song.

At last the little girl opened her eyes with amazement
and wonder at the world of sunshine she'd been brought
into. Then Paulette took the child into her heart where she
would always be safe. The abandoned child within
started to grow up.

We are safe as long as we don't abandon ourselves.

Jenny, like so many people, had grown up believing
she had no rights. Because she felt she was worthless she
naturally couldn't stand up for herself, so she constantly
tried to please people.

All the men she related to treated her badly and she
accepted it, believing that was her role in life.

I asked her to look within to see where she had given
her power away.

She saw herself as a three year old, surrounded by
shimmering energy and power. When her brother was
born, she was full of jealousy. She felt her power would be
overwhelming if she let go control.

I asked her how she coped with the power, (in other
words the feelings) and she saw that she had bandaged
herself up with it. Then she bound the rest of the power
up and buried it under a tree in the garden.

And as she realised what she had done to herself, she
saw herself release the child and dig up the rest of the
bindings.

Then she asked the child how she could handle her life
so that she could keep her power. The child said, 'I can let
it flow into me like a great heat and light', and she threw
her arms open wide and felt and saw the power coming
back into her. She absorbed the now powerful child into
herself.

Jenny visualised herself handling her new power. She was able to say 'No' quite clearly, especially to men. She could set her boundaries and assert her rights.

For Jenny it was another small step towards finding herself. She had many other inner children to rescue.

All greed, jealousy, hurt, anger and any other bad feelings are held at the level of the inner child.

When you become aware of feelings of anger or thoughts of jealousy, try to imagine yourself as a child with those feelings. See yourself as that child who first held those feelings. Rescue yourself. Give yourself the comfort and love you wanted then.

If an incident flashes to mind in connection with an emotion, imagine you are helping the child to deal with the incident with confidence. Let the child inside you express its needs and pent up emotions. Comfort and love and heal the incident. You may like to take your inner child to some runnng water to 'cleanse' the incident in the mind. All symbolic work helps to reinforce messages and healings in the inner mind.

ELEVEN

Healing the Wounded Child

All young creatures need tender, loving encouragement. If you knew a puppy which was constantly scolded, beaten, kicked and put out in the cold, you wouldn't be at all surprised if it grew into a skulking, cowering, whining dog – or a snappy untrustworthy animal.

You'd probably feel rightly indignant and think its owner deserved all he got if the dog turned on him.

People know instinctively that puppies need love and encouragement to grow into confident, alert, responsive dogs.

If you have a delicate seedling, you plant it carefully in suitable soil. You water it, feed it, put it in sun or shade according to its needs and delight as it responds and grows into a healthy plant, covered in bloom.

If you plant it in poor soil in a part of the garden where it is constantly trampled on, it will either die or become a miserable non-flowering plant. You'll never know what it could have become.

And small children are exactly the same. If you constantly nag at your child, find fault with him, get angry with him, threaten him, smack him, what do you expect?

He may cower away from people. He won't trust himself to do anything right. He'll be too frightened and confused to try anything new. He'll sit at the back of the classroom and never learn. He daren't trust others or life itself. He gives up.

Or he may rebel and, like the dog who snarls and growls and bites, he'll become rude, defiant and aggressive.

Quite likely he'll respond in a bit of both ways.

If your child is just getting onto his feet and learning to walk, do you knock him over, ridicule him and tell him he's stupid when he stumbles?

Of course not. You hold your arms out to catch him. You praise each step. You tell him how clever he is. You encourage him all the time. When he gets steadier you stand by to pick him up when he falls. You comfort him and encourage him to try again. Soon he feels safe enough to pick himself up and walk again with increasing confidence.

He beams with delight at his success and when he falls, his misery is short lived.

He learns that, however many times he fails, he is still loved and accepted. He realises it is alright to try and fail because he can try again until he succeeds.

This means he learns to trust himself and others. He dares to try new things and still feel good about himself if he fails. And Life is a learning experience. To grow we must attempt the new. To evolve we must dare to experience.

Most of us are very hard on ourselves. We don't realise we are beating and battering our fragile, sensitive inner child.

How do you treat yourself? Do you batter and discourage your inner child? Do you criticize yourself? Do you hold yourself back? Do you dwell on your weaknesses?

Or do you praise and encourage yourself? Do you look for your good points and enhance them? Do you build on your strengths?

If we repeatedly tell ourselves we are no good, we are discouraging our inner child.

Suppose you decide to give up sweets or cigarettes or to change a habit. If you lapse, do you criticize yourself bitterly and order yourself to do better next time?

Your child could well be rebelling against your tyranny – like the dog who turns and bites his master. Or your child may feel so hopelessly doomed to failure that it gives up.

Either way, being hard on ourselves is not helping. We are making life very difficult and discouraging.

Befriend your child. Love yourself. Accept yourself. Praise your good qualities. Encourage yourself. Then watch yourself grow into a beautiful person.

You will grow and bloom as surely as the little plant when it is watered and nourished and no longer trampled upon.

You will feel safer, more trusting and more confident in yourself.

This is how it worked for a friend of mine who is a keen tennis player. She normally played an excellent game but when I watched her one evening she was very much off form. Her confidence was visibly slipping away as she misjudged the ball repeatedly. She lost the first set disastrously.

She walked slowly to the other end and paused, as if in deep thought, before the second set started. She almost visibly relaxed and her game picked up dramatically during the remainder of the match.

After the game I asked her how she had done it. She smiled and said, 'I just told myself I was a wonderful person whatever the outcome of the match. I reminded myself that I had won lots of matches and am a really good player. This helped me to relax so I could remember how to play well. It always does the trick'.

When we really love, accept and encourage our inner child, we can never harm ourselves or anyone else. Only hurt people hurt others.

Tough, dynamic businessmen often react with disbelief when I talk to them about their inner child. To be easy on themselves is so different from the thrusting control they so often impose on themselves.

One such man, Douglas, came to me with a lack of confidence when talking to his bosses and clients, manifesting in hesitancy of speech. And this is very common.

We worked together for two sessions and he was feeling much more confident. I felt he needed to contact the little child within him who had not been allowed to express himself freely.

When I asked him to see himself as a child, he could see nothing but mist. We tried for some time but nothing came and I thought he was going to block the healing.

Suddenly the mist cleared for him and he met himself as a child – vulnerable, hurt and put down. Instinctively he drew the little Douglas into his arms and gave him the comfort and encouragement and praise he so much needed as a four year old. He promised the child he was safe with him and that from now on he'd always try to understand how he felt, so that he could trust him. He gave the child permission to talk and express himself clearly.

He was amazed when he opened his eyes. He said that he felt that he was in touch with himself for the first time ever.

The awareness came to him that as a child he'd been told so often to be quiet that he'd given away his power to speak freely. In the meeting with his child he reclaimed the power. He told me later that when he met himself, he felt it was an incredible breakthrough in his life, as since then he'd felt at peace.

Many people claim that they had a wonderful child-hood and their parents both loved them (as they undoubt-edly did). They can't understand why they feel so ill or unhappy as adults, and hurt and rejected by little things.

One such person was Frieda, a widow, who came from a large family of brothers and sisters. She had several children and numerous grandchildren. She was desper-ately possessive. Her mind seethed with bitter jealousy and anger against everyone in her life. She felt put upon, ignored and taken for granted. She constantly complained that no one took any notice of how she felt.

Her body was protesting with all sorts of physical symptoms. She always assured me that her parents loved her and her siblings and session after session we peeled away layers. When I asked her to see herself as a little girl who had to give away her sense of identity, her self worth and sense of value, she found herself at five years old. She was crouching in a corner. I asked her what the five year old child wanted and she gasped 'I don't believe it'. A long pause ensured. At last she sighed. 'She says she wants to be loved. I always thought she was.'

When she had fulfilled the inner child's need for love, she opened her eyes and we talked.

Frieda was the oldest girl in the family and when she was five years old her mother had twins. As the 'responsible' one, Frieda had to look after her numerous brothers, who teased her unmercifully.

No one valued or appreciated her for herself. She grew up with a firmly embedded belief that the only justification for her existence was to care for others. No wonder she had so many children and was so possessive of them. No wonder she let herself be put down. If her children freed themselves from her, where was her justification for being alive.

She constantly recreated that feeling she had as a five year old. Her work is to love that child and return her self respect.

Some years ago there was a person in my life who really irritated me. We were thrown together in a group every week and I couldn't understand why it was I felt so uncomfortable with her.

So I meditated on the problem between us. I saw her as a child kicking and screaming for help and getting all the attention.

I as a child stood by watching her. I desperately wanted attention too. However I'd learnt as a child that I must not kick or scream as I would be rejected, so I put down my feelings. I was being ignored and I did not know how to get the attention I wanted. So I felt frustrated and angry inside.

I realised that this was exactly what was happening whenever I saw her in the group. In her way she was screaming for attention and getting it. I wanted to scream for attention too but, because of my early learnings, had to control my feelings. What I experienced was the helpless frustration and anger of my inner child.

With this came the awareness that I needed to do much more work with my inner child. My inner child needed to be helped to feel so comfortable with herself that she didn't have to demand so much attention. She also needed to learn to ask for the attention she did need in a more appropriate way. As I accepted the lesson I'd been given, this person floated out of my life.

If you feel depressed or irritable in gatherings where other people are getting attention, look at the needs of your inner child.

Frustration, irritation, depression, all the annoyance we feel with certain people and in certain situations all tell us that there is something within us which needs to be looked at. Those certain people and situations are our teachers giving us the chance to learn. The Universe will always supply teachers for what we are working on within ourselves or for what we need to work on.

When I was getting divorced my relationship with my parents was very bad. I felt angry, hurt, bitter and on the defensive. For me divorce was failure. I had failed as a woman, as a mother. I felt not good enough, rejected, not lovable. My parents twisted knives in all my wounds and I couldn't handle my inner pain, so I withdrew and didn't visit them any more. I kept telling myself I'd work on my feelings when I felt stronger.

Then I met someone at a workshop who looked exactly like my mother. I role played the situation in my life with her as my mother. Excruciating pains came up in my chest. I went home feeling terrible. All night I felt knives being twisted in my heart. I did not sleep.

Next morning a friend called in and I told her what had happened. At once she said, 'Go inside and see what is in there'. So I closed my eyes and focused on the pain in my chest.

I saw in my chest a black target full of barbed arrows. One by one I started to pull them out, but this was slow and painful, so eventually I grabbed a handful. As I tugged the whole target swung open as if on a hinge and I could see steps disappearing into the darkness below.

Down and down I climbed until I came to a dimly lit corridor. Again I walked seemingly for miles but there was a light at the end, so I knew I was heading in the right direction.

There in a little room at the end of the corridor was a small terrified child, whom I recognised as my mother.

She was so terrified that she was shooting arrows all around her to keep everyone away.

I called softly to her until she paused and then I went up to her and put my arms around her and comforted her. When she stopped crying I surrounded her with pink light.

At that instant everything went black. Then I saw the target in the sky with light pouring through the holes where I'd pulled the arrows out.

I opened my eyes. The pain in my chest had gone – and I had a new awareness of what was happening in my mother's inner world.

Stress, tension, anxiety and all forms of fear, together with the angry, jealous, hurt, mean feelings we have, are based on the fear of the inner child.

So when you feel hurt or angry, visualise the small child within you and sense what the underlying basis of the fear is. Is it the fear of failure, fear of rejection, fear of not living up to expectations? Is it a fear that you'll never get your needs met or will never be heard? Talk to your inner child. Listen to it. What does it have to say? What does it need? When it feels safe enough to be honest, you may be surprised at what it tells you about yourself.

Reassure your child. Comfort it. Love it. Start working together. It is much pleasanter and easier to walk the path of life with a child who is happy and co-operative, than carrying one who is kicking and screaming, protesting or even half dead. That is a burden indeed to carry through life.

Hear your child. Respect it. When you hear and respect your inner child, you will respect yourself, so the world will respect you.

All aspects of you will be working together and you will no longer slightly out of synch with yourself. You will give out an impression of harmony.

TWELVE

The Healing Power of Forgiveness

May was a well groomed, highly intelligent blonde. Only a tightness to her lips and an edge to her voice detracted from her good looks. She had many friends but she was lonely. Her two marriages had ended in divorce.

She was aware that she was creating a great deal of pain and unhappiness for herself and wanted to understand why.

As a young child her parents had abandoned her, first to a children's home and then to a relative. She had never seen her mother since that dreadful day when she'd toddled into the children's home and her mother had never returned.

May bitterly described her mother as immature and only interested in herself.

Her father she described with equal acrimony as totally selfish. Their callous rejection of her left deep grief-filled wounds within her and she was very bitter against them.

We worked to validate the wounded child within her. Then we examined her parents' background in order that she could understand the fear that lay under their immaturity and selfishness – a fear so deep that they abandoned their child. May began to realise how her parents' deep inner fears drove them to behave as they did. Compassion stirred within her. 'I've never thought of what they were going through', she murmured, looking softer.

She visualised each of her parents as children with their own fears, so enormous that they couldn't cope.

And then she forgave them from the bottom of her heart. As she did so she saw herself standing in a meadow beaming them up into her heart. Then she suddenly saw herself transforming into a huge, beautiful butterfly.

She looked radiant.

When we cannot forgive, we are judging another. The Law says, 'Judge not lest you be judged'. To blame or to criticise another or ourself is to judge. When true forgiveness is in our hearts we are all one.

It's not only relationships that need to be forgiven. People who are subjected to assaults or robberies or who have been cheated often carry anger and bitter unforgiveness in their hearts.

Beryl devoted her life to others. She was a lovely person and yet she felt worthless. Because she undervalued herself she let herself be put on and put down. And she let the hurt squeeze the joy from her heart, so that she gave herself angina.

I liked Beryl tremendously. Despite her terrible feelings of pain and hurt, she had an inner knowing that she was doing it all to herself and was ready to take responsibility but didn't know how to.

For her sensitive spirit she had undertaken a difficult path in this life and was eager to open up her heart and let go of the grudges and bitterness. She had always been a 'nice' person, willing to please everyone and it isn't easy for 'nice' people to admit that they hold grudges and bitterness. She was opening out beautifully and letting go of all sorts of negativities.

Then she had a setback. Her holiday caravan had been broken into and vandalised. She came to see me ten days later, bitter, upset, shaky and churning.

A few days after the incident a feeling had told her to go to the caravan and sit outside it in her car. Soon she noticed two young men staring at her. She 'knew' it was them. They felt evil to her and she found herself so shaky with rage and fear that she couldn't move.

At last she drove home. Her angina was so bad that she couldn't even tell the police as she feared she'd have a heart attack.

As she told me about it she could feel her heart racing. 'I just can't forgive them. They're evil', she declared. However she wanted to clear her own pain and so she agreed to see what we could do.

She closed her eyes. I asked her to imagine the two youths as small children and try to imagine what had happened for them to make them as they were.

She saw the two little boys wanting to hurt others because they had been so hurt. She could sense them being emotionally rejected and finding security and revenge from the things they grabbed from others.

She felt a great pity for them welling up inside her.

I asked her to open up her heart and dissolve all her angry feelings with gold. Then I suggested she imagine herself putting her arms around the youths.

She started to chuckle and said, 'They wouldn't like that but I'm doing it all the same', and her whole face transformed as the anger and fear she'd been holding in her heart dissolved. She forgave them.

The pain in her heart left. The tension in her body relaxed. She realised how much she'd been hurting herself as she kept chuckling to herself at the memory of the youths' faces when she put her arms round them.

When we forgive another we heal our pain.

There are times when a person isn't ready to forgive or perhaps pays lip service to forgiveness, so that the stone is still there in his heart.

If we are not ready to forgive, then we have to wait until more understanding, compassion and wisdom flow in – and until that happens we will continue to punish ourselves with anger or bitterness or tension. We will continue to give ourselves ulcers, heart attacks, gall bladder problems and many other symptoms.

Occasionally someone will say he thinks he's forgiven but he's not sure. If he has forgiven and really let go of the hurt then his body will feel different. The person or event causing the pain becomes a memory like any other memory, no longer charged with emotion. He will be able to meet the other person as if the situation had never happened between them.

When we express the willingness to forgive we are taking a major step towards letting go.

When someone cannot forgive, I sometimes ask them to look down on the situation on earth from a higher perspective. Very often the low earthbound self cannot forgive but the Higher Self, when called upon, will always do so.

Barry had always had throat problems. He held a belief that it was not safe to express himself.

His relationship with his wife was fraught and he blamed it on her shouting at the children, which made him cross. Because she was often irritable and upset, Barry was sure that this was affecting the children badly.

When the children were very small he had remonstrated with his wife but this had served to make her even more irritable and upset, so that she shouted at the children more than ever. So Barry decided he couldn't win and had better swallow his anger and keep quiet. He placed himself in the position of confirming his belief that it was not safe to express himself.

As we looked at the situation he could see that his anger, whether expressed or unexpressed, was creating a wall between himself and his wife. The wall was his anger, and the root cause of his anger was the fear that he couldn't safely say what he wanted to. His wife attacked the invisible wall with all the verbal and emotional weapons she possessed, from her fear that she couldn't get through to him.

Barry worked to release the fear that it wasn't safe to express himself. He immediately saw his heart open and dissolve the wall with love. Without his wall to block him in he was able to radiate love to his wife.

He saw that as he no longer had a wall around himself, she had nothing to attack. Her sniping stopped when he saw himself dissolve with love all the shots she was sending. In his inner scene he saw himself return all the shots she fired at him as little golden balls of love.

Up to that moment the sniping and attacking shots she had fired had of course been boomeranging back straight at her. And now as her attacks were returned with an energy of love, Barry saw her transform into a different person.

He continued to watch his inner scene and saw that the bullets had also been ricocheting towards his children. As these ricochets ceased, his children's walls of fear dissolved and they laughed in delight and relief.

He had been blaming his wife for his problems and now he could see how he was responsible for his share of creating the situation. He was able to forgive her and himself and know that there was hope of healing the home situation.

When we blame others we are defending or attacking from fear.

Everything we give out boomerangs back to us. When we send out fear or anger it comes back to hit us. However if we radiate love, it absorbs and dissolves the nastiness from another. Then the boomerang effect doesn't take place.

We can thus help others to transmute their fears with our love.

Many people hold a deep unforgiving rage about being bullied at school. I've often heard people say that it is totally wicked and unforgivable and has ruined their life.

Nancy felt that her school days had been totally destroyed by the girls at school who bullied her in a variety of ways.

She felt small and weak and vulnerable. She also felt different from everyone else. She was afraid of rejection and of being destroyed by the bigger girls. Her feeling of being different kept her apart from everyone else.

Those big bullying girls were afraid too.

Nancy closed her eyes and saw herself as the little vulnerable girl. She saw that the wall of fear she had around her was thick and impenetrably black.

When she looked into the eyes of the bullies she saw that they were afraid too – afraid of her rejection of them all, afraid they could never get her to like them, afraid because she perceived herself as different and anyone who is different is a threat.

Nancy realised that she held the same fears as they did.

They had defended themselves by attacking her.

I asked her to open her heart. Nancy immediately saw gold light flowing from her body and dissolving her wall of fear. At that the fear left the faces of the bullies and they all opened their arms to her to accept her with love.

Her fear attracted the bullying. As she became aware she forgave them and forgave herself and she felt a hard knot dissolve in her stomach.

Phillip had been cheated out of his life savings by a partner. He had to sell his house and he was frantic with rage and worry. He was also a very old soul and an aware man.

He realised that it was a lesson and that he couldn't have been cheated unless he was cheating too.

It was not too difficult for him to be aware that he was cheating emotionally, lying to himself and others about his feelings. He also saw that he was cheating himself by wanting so much to believe in his partner that he turned a blind eye to all the evidence.

He accepted that he had to learn to trust his intuition and value himself.

He experienced that he had let similar situations arise with the same man in other lives because he had again hoodwinked himself – and he had not learnt the lessons.

I explained that the money he had lost represented the exact amount of energy he had cheated himself by. He had already recognised that. I explained money came from God and was not controlled by us. That particular money was lost but if he let go of the anger about the money he could open himself up again for more.

A few weeks later he said, 'I'm ready now to let go of the money. I recognise that enormous benefits have come to me through this misfortune.

'I now have friends and interests I'd never have had without it. People have been supportive in a way I'd never have believed and paradoxically it has renewed my faith in human nature.'

I took him into his inner world and we did an exercise to release the money he had lost, with love. He let it go easily and felt a physical lifting. Then he totally forgave the man who had cheated him. When he opened his eyes, he said, 'It's as if that man and I were one'.

That's true forgiveness.

His aches and pains vanished and he knew inside himself that he'd cleared a major hurdle and all was well in his life.

THIRTEEN

Healing Relationships

More stress and pain is caused by relationship problems than anything else.

We all know people who complain and grumble about their mother, father, workmates, relatives, friends, neighbours, children. The moaner is being a victim, who has given the other person power to make them angry or upset.

When we are whole people, we take responsibility for our own power.

No one can make us angry unless we let them.

No one can upset us unless we've allowed them to hook into a weakness within us.

No one has the power to hurt us. We can only hurt ourselves.

If someone needs to throw a dart or brick, it is his problem. It is only ours if we let it affect us. Bounce it back with love.

Usually someone says, 'What if he pushes me over and breaks my leg?'

The answer is that the leg heals. The real hurt is caused by the churning thoughts, the vindictive angry brooding feelings and emotions. They can even prevent the leg from healing.

Nothing can hurt us but our thoughts.

Brooding thoughts are very different from talking or acting out a trauma as it actually occurred. When we talk or act out something traumatic, the energy charge of fear is released so that inner healing can take place.

So if we are involved in a trauma what can we do? If it keeps occurring in our minds and we cannot exorcise it, it helps to talk it out with someone and express the feelings. If our friends and family are bored with hearing about it, we may need to go to a counsellor.

We must beware of turning a natural need to exorcise feelings into wallowing.

If a person has done us an injustice we have a choice. We can choose to brood angrily or wallow in self pity, or both. This harms us. It harms our body. It destroys our peace and adds to the negative energy cloud in the Universe.

Or we can decide to choose peace and forgiveness. We choose our thoughts.

So what can we do when we feel hurt?

We can consciously decide to let the anger pass and choose peace and forgiveness.

Then we can look at what was going on inside us that attracted the accident or trauma into our life.

Whenever Ann saw her mother she churned with anger and misery for days, so that her neck would ache and her head throb. Mention her mother and Ann's fists and jaw would tighten.

Her mother would constantly harp on about how wonderful Ann's brother was and how he'd achieved this and that and done so well.

Ann was holding down a responsible job and was a single parent with two children.

Her mother's comments about her brother were hooking into Ann's inner feelings about being merely a girl and not good enough. Up rose the helpless frustration and rage of the two year old who could never compete against her older brother. However hard the two year old tried, she could never be as good as her brother. And she'd been battling the unequal fight ever since.

Ann started working on herself, affirming that she was valuable, worthwhile and happy to be a woman. As she accepted and healed herself, she began to feel more comfortable inside. So her mother's comments no longer wounded her. She no longer needed to be on the defensive with her mother. Their relationship became more open and comfortable.

As they relaxed together, Ann's mother stopped talking incessantly about her brother because she no longer had to batter Ann's defences to get in. Ann felt safe enough within herself to let down the drawbridge and welcome her mother in.

Comments about her wonderful brother no longer had any power to make her angry.

Peter had a very similar problem. His mother constantly praised and talked about his successful brother, leaving Peter depressed and raw each time he saw her. He would have a sore throat after every visit.

He knew that his brother felt equally uptight after seeing his mother and so we examined why it was that his mother needed to upset them both.

Peter had a lot of insight about his mother's childhood. He realised that she had learnt to set her parents one against the other to maintain control and get attention for herself. She still did it. She was now trying to split her sons to retain control and power.

Because her parents used to put her down as a child, her learnings were that that's what parents did to children. That was the only way she knew to handle Peter and his brother. So she subtly put each son down by praising the other. It is a common form of family manipulation.

Peter worked to build his self esteem. At the same time he recognised in his mother the fearful child, desperately trying to control the people in her life. He could see her need for attention and her deep need to be loved and accepted.

He found it easy to feel compassion for the needy, fearful child in his mother. With the understanding and compassion came warmth and forgiveness.

He let go of his antagonism towards her and as his attitude changed, he dealt tenderly with his mother's inner child. He no longer gave her the power to upset him. As his mother felt safe and comfortable with him, she relaxed and the relationship began to heal.

Polly was the youngest child of a large family. With so much competition she had to fight for her share of everything – love, attention, goodies. She had learnt to be watchful constantly, in case she missed out or was put upon.

Naturally she learnt various strategies to get her needs met. She learnt that if she sulked or went quiet someone would coax her out of it. She would get the attention she craved and sometimes the goodies as well.

Other times she would be screaming and demanding. She got attention this way too, and sometimes the goodies to keep her quiet. Sometimes she got a smack but nevertheless it was attention.

She married a man who had been rejected by his mother. This man was going to test his wife's love in every possible way to see if she too would reject him. So he provoked and tested her constantly, by being late, untidy, lazy. He tried everything.

Her learnings were that if she gave in over anything, she'd be taken advantage. of. Then she'd be powerless. She could let nothing pass. She sulked or raged and demanded. They were locked in a power struggle over everything. So they quarrelled incessantly.

He couldn't make it up because he was re-living the feelings of his mother rejecting him. She couldn't make it up in case she lost her power.

They had evolved a ritual whereby, after each quarrel, both would withdraw into silence. Then one would touch the other, who would reject the overture. Later the other would advance and touch, also to be rejected. On the third occasion, when one made the move, they would wordlessly accept the end of the quarrel. The whole procedure could take hours or even days and nothing was resolved. It was a nerve wracking, emotionally exhausting process.

They were like two knights in armour fighting each other when actually they were on the same side.

It only needed one to drop the sword and refuse to strike back. The other would no longer fight an unarmed opponent. Then they could take off their armour, which is cumbersome and unnecessary in peace and in marriage, and work together for the same cause – their relationship.

Polly was very scared of being vulnerable when she dropped her sword – and she often picked up and struck back. But she soon learnt that her husband was so disarmed when, in response to his provocation, she smiled acceptingly instead of retaliating, that she gradually felt safe enough to drop her weapons completely.

He naturally soon followed suit.

When we meet attack with counter attack the result is war. When we meet attack with a gesture of peace, the result is peace.

When Suzie first came to see me she told me bitterly that her mother was a weak, lazy, neurotic woman. Her father was a mean, domineering bully and a real male chauvinist pig. She said, 'male chauvinist pig' through clenched teeth. Both were totally materialistic, she claimed, and emotionally blocked.

She continued to chronicle her family. Her aunt was a harpy, her grandmother an interfering busybody, her brother Mum's golden boy, her sister Dad's pet who could do no wrong.

Relationships were so bad that she rarely saw her family.

Her work was unfulfilling and she thought her colleagues were boring, small minded people.

She blamed and criticised everyone and felt so threatened by life and people that she looked for slights and insults in everything.

Suzie had no friends. The only person in the world she felt safe with was her husband.

Now Suzie did a remarkable thing during that first session. I explained how we created our lives, and in one magic moment she took responsibility for what she had created. She made the awareness. In that instant she transformed from helpless victim to mistress of her destiny, only needing help to understand why she felt as she did and how to transform those feelings.

She saw that she and her husband had locked themselves into the safety of a fortress, from which they attacked the world. It was cold and dark in there.

Using imagery she knocked down the walls of the fortress and stepped out into the world of sunshine. She rescued, healed and loved many aspects of her inner child. She understood why her parents responded as they did.

We went through her life looking at, understanding, releasing and forgiving all the hurtful people and events she had encountered.

Everything we worked on in our sessions, she took home and discussed with her husband. They worked together with imagery, mirror work, affirmations and exercises I gave them.

The couple became outgoing and friendly. They were astonished and delighted when both sets of parents responded by being friendly and extremely generous.

They joined a club and found everyone warm and helpful. They started to invite people into their home. Suzie told me she couldn't believe how many nice people there were around. She gave up her job and immediately found a congenial one which used her talents. Her confidence increased. She glowed. She became fulfilled and warm and friendly.

The world hadn't changed. Only her perception of it. She created a new reality for herself.

Our inner world creates our outer world. Our subjective world creates our objective world.

I knew a lady who annoyed me intensely. One day in meditation, I saw this aggravating woman walking towards me.

Suddenly I saw her body break in two like a walnut shell and split apart. A beautiful golden lady emerged and smiled at me. We walked hand in hand to a waterfall and stood under it together. I was being made aware of her Higher Self and shown that even while two people are fighting or thinking acrimonious thoughts of each other, their Higher Selves are standing by watching and holding hands.

Only the part of us that is blocked off from love needs to fight.

It is only our lower selves which quarrel. Our Higher Selves are always at one.

FOURTEEN

The Heart Centre

On the day of the Harmonic Convergence I was with friends meditating on a local hill at sunrise. The sun appeared as a magnificent ball of pure gold; the grass, the trees, our bodies were glowing with golden light.

It was easy to be in harmony when bathed in that light. a voice in my head said, 'Relax and Trust', and I knew it to be my message. An amazing sense of peace filled my heart.

Next day we returned to meditate again on the hilltop at sunrise. This time a bank of mist obliterated the sun – but the sun was still there. The only difference was that we could not see or feel it.

It was then an act of faith to believe it was there.

Our heart centres are like the sun, a huge radiant golden ball of light. Negative thoughts are the clouds that cross it. A few negative thoughts are barely noticeable wisps, while dreadful fears, angers, jealousies build a huge cloud bank which obliterates the light. It is from these dark clouds that the rain, snow and hail drop into our lives.

Yet, whatever passes over it or blocks it out, the sun is always there. When we accept that the sun is always there in our heart centre and that we alone block the light out with our negativities, we recognise how important it is to clear away those clouds.

Trusting that the sun is indeed behind the clouds, waiting to shine into our life, is the first step.

Accepting that each and every thought and belief that blocks our peace and happiness is our own cloud, created by us, is the second.

Being willing to let go of the hurt or fear or anger is the third.

I often find clouds blocking out the sun in my heart. Sometimes a series of great black clouds obliterate the sunlight and I know I have to take decisions to look within and see where they come from. I must decide whether I would rather hold onto this anger or release it and clear that cloud away.

Anger is often connected with the fear that a person will again do something to hurt us. Yet if we hold onto the anger we will re-create the situation and ensure that we will be hurt again. The only way to prevent ourselves being hurt any more is to let the anger cloud float away.

The longer we hold onto resentment and bitterness the more deeply embedded within us they become.

It sometimes feels impossible to clear the hurt when a loved one seems to be rejecting us. The more we churn it over, the blacker and deeper it becomes. We may have undertaken to clear that hurt many lifetimes ago and are putting ourselves through the same pain again and again until we learn that only our ego self can be hurt. Our spiritual being is love. It is timeless and eternal and cannot be hurt or die.

Our creator is perfect. We are part of our creator. Therefore we must be perfect. Only fears held by our ego self create the clouds which block out this Truth.

Louise looked twenty years older than her chronological age. Her son never wrote to her and her father preferred her sister. She spent all her energy brooding about her son and sending angry thoughts to her father and sister. She did everything for her father, trying to gain his love and attention. She wooed him like a wife, chased him and tried to ingratiate herself. At the same time she made herself ill with frustration and rage.

No wonder there was darkness and thunder in her life. She created great clouds which blocked out her sun. She couldn't recognise that she was perfect so she couldn't clear away the clouds.

It took a great deal of work on herself before she caught glimpses of the sun and let it start to shine in her life.

The heart is the centre of our being. When we are at peace and in harmony the sun is shining in our lives. We are centred.

Throughout the ages the heart has symbolised love. The heart is the love centre because this is where the divine light is held within us. When our heart centre opens we are opening to our Higher Selves.

When our heart centre is wide open, a pure light is radiating around us and nothing can come in to harm us, because there is nothing within to attract harm. *When we radiate only love and goodwill, we are centred in a golden aura. This is the armour of God.*

Our fears and hurts and barriers block our heart centres, cutting us off from the source of Power, Light and Inspiration.

We talk of someone being warm hearted, kind hearted, soft hearted, cold hearted, mean hearted or hard hearted. We say one has a heart of gold and another a heart of ice.

I sometimes ask clients to visualise what is happening in their heart centre. Their inner mind will give them a symbolic picture which reveals what their conscious mind may not acknowledge.

Linda was brown haired and brown eyed and her eyes held a slightly withdrawn look, for she had experienced a loveless childhood. Her husband complained that she was an iceberg and she agreed. She said, 'I don't want to be cold but I know I am. I just ice up somehow'.

I asked her to close her eyes and relax and then she allowed an image of her heart to appear. Indeed she saw a lump of ice. We let the sun shine on to the ice to melt it. Slowly drip by drip, the ice began to melt. It was a long process.

Her chest hurt with the pain of the ice melting but she continued to let the sun thaw the ice, until there, deep inside the lump of ice lay a soft pink heart.

Her eyes shone when she opened them and she felt she'd achieved something really important.

She agreed to relax twice a day and visualise the sun melting the ice around her heart until her next appointment, which was a month later.

And a month later when I opened the door it was as if a different person stood there. Her eyes were gentler, her hair was softer, her jaw line had relaxed. She said it was the most painful month of her life but she'd done the exercises every day because she knew how important it was.

Her husband was amazed at the change in Linda, but then she was symbolically giving herself a very powerful message to change.

Shona had never married nor had a satisfactory relationship with a man, though she very much wanted to. Her attitude to men was wary because of the relationship she'd had with her father, who constantly undermined her confidence. But she was a kind woman and a dedicated nurse.

When she visualised her heart, she was horrified to find that it was covered in pus and she set to work with a will to scrub it all off. When it was cleansed, she painted it outside and inside in a fresh soft pink. When the centre of her being seemed soft and clean and welcoming, she opened it all up to let in light and friendships.

'It's no wonder I haven't got a man,' she said quietly and thoughtfully.

She worked daily with her heart cleaning and began to feel much more at peace. She also made more friendships, but when I last saw her, she wasn't yet ready to attract a relationship.

Henry was in the middle of marital turmoil. He fluctuated between anger, panic and self-pity, and was going round in circles.

He arrived on time for one session and threw himself into the chair. 'I shouldn't have come', he moaned. 'I feel dreadful. I've got flu. I'm stuffed up and I've got a temperature and I ache all over.'

His body was responding to the chaotic messages he was sending from his mind.

He agreed to do a heart visualisation and after we'd cut away the barbed wire which he saw tangled round his heart, he opened the door to his heart and gasped.

The inside was full of maggots. After the initial shock

he took a broom and began to sweep them out. When every one had gone, he scrubbed out his heart and decorated it, then furnished the room in a soft welcoming way, and put in fresh flowers, lit candles and made his heart into a place of peace.

He had certainly given his inner mind clear instructions, because when he opened his eyes, he laughed and sprang from the chair. 'I don't need to be ill now. I feel wonderful!'

To follow your heart not your head is wisdom. The Law of Intuition says that when you follow your inner guidance, which means when you listen to your heart, you will be on the right pathway.

This is what happened to Yvonne when she tuned into her heart. She was a thin, anxious lady, always ready to help others but desperately unhappy. Every muscle in her body was tense and aching and she was constantly at the doctor's surgery.

Her problem was that her children took her for granted and her husband was totally disinterested in her. She wanted so much to be a good wife and mother, but her anger and frustration, her bitterness and hurt, made her feel inadequate and guilty.

By the time she came to see me, she felt she hated her husband. She brooded over every slight and hurt. Her head said she should leave him and seek happiness elsewhere. To her intense amazement, when she looked inside her heart, there quietly sat her husband.

At that instant, she decided to use all the energy she had been using in hating him into understanding and cementing the relationship. Each day she visualised him inside her heart with love, which was giving her inner computer messages to look for ways of healing their marriage.

Over the next weeks all her pains and tension fell away as the home situation transformed. By acting on her heart's message, in other words trusting her intuition, she found love.

When we really take a decision to move forward on our pathway, the Universe will give us every help to grow by providing us with suitable opportunities and tests.

Amanda had to justify her very existence, her womanhood, her right to breathe. Her guilt about being alive was enormous.

Not surprisingly, her marriage was unsuccessful. She tried to be a perfect wife and mother, hold down a job and expect herself to succeed one hundred per cent in each area. Her anger against her family for not recognising her needs was enormous.

I took her in to see what was blocking her heart and she started to cry. There, standing with arms and legs outstretched, blocking the entrance, was a man. She sobbed that years ago he'd been her lover for a few weeks and she'd never told anyone. She thought she had blotted it from her mind.

She agreed to release and heal the guilt from that relationship by cleansing him and herself in running water and forgiving him for his part in what had happened. In her mind she asked her husband's forgiveness and received it. She had more difficulty in forgiving herself. In our arrogance we are always much harder on ourselves. We expect more of ourselves forgetting we are here to experience and to learn.

However she did at last forgive herself unconditionally and the lover departed, leaving her free to look into her heart and find her family there.

She reported that her relationship with her husband had improved immediately. Her guilt had been the barrier to their love. Because of her guilt she had forced herself to repay by undertaking far too much. Now she was able to cut down on her work hours and to allow herself to enjoy her home. It wasn't long after that that her husband was offered the chance of a move so that she no longer had any reminders of her guilt. As she released her guilt, the Universe stepped in to help by letting her move away from the memories.

We all put ourselves through so much unnecessary suffering. When I look back on my life I can wonder a million times why couldn't I have been more philosophical, or why didn't I accept the inevitable, or did I really have to feel so guilty or why hadn't I tried to understand how the other felt and let my feelings go.

Liz had put herself through so much panic and fear that she couldn't leave the house. Her palpitations became so bad that she thought she would have a heart attack.

She was a highly intelligent and articulate woman – a real thinker and intellectualiser. I looked at her as she sat tense and rigid in the chair and wondered how I could help her to let go. She told me that she never relaxed, couldn't sleep and was always rigid with tension.

She was so wary that she wouldn't even close her eyes for more than a moment. Eventually I persuaded her to close her eyes to see if she could imagine what was round her heart, squeezing it so hard.

I think she was more intrigued than expecting anything to happen. She closed her eyes and I asked her to visualise her heart in front of her and see what was squeezing it. She murmured in surprise, 'There are hands round it, holding it tight.'

Liz took longer to see whose hands they were and then she gasped in astonishment. 'They're my own hands. I'm going to get them away.' It was quite a struggle but as her hands came away from her heart, she suddenly relaxed. Her breathing slowed down, her tension fell away and she went into a comfortable trance state, so that we were able to start inner work.

She began to experience life without the palpitations she'd been giving herself. Using the power of her imagination she began to heal herself. Soon she was sleeping and driving again.

Every cell has life and intelligence. Each stores memories and radiates an energy. Plants, rocks, minerals, everything radiates an electro-magnetic field which can be photographed by Kirlian photography. If you have green fingers you don't need to be told that you are communicating that certain something with your plants. If you go into nature and feel at peace, you are receiving peaceful energy from nature. If the sea energises you, you are receiving from that element.

After the hurricane in England, many sensitive people

were feeling peculiarly upset. They were responding to the anguished cries from the trees, which were torn and hurt.

I was once talking to a friend on the phone. He said something which I perceived as hurtful and I immediately saw a chain and padlock go round my heart and click shut. I debated within myself whether or not to sit down and visualise it coming off but decided I needed that protection at that moment.

I stayed at a friend's house that weekend and woke early, so I lay in bed and sent love to all my plants at home. As I did so I saw cupped hands below my beautiful hanging fern. I watched intrigued as energy from all the plants in the house radiated to the fern and was collected in the cupped hands.

Then the hands opened towards me lying in bed fifty miles away and the energy flow of love towards my heart shattered apart the padlock and chain. My plants were returning the love I sent them – and with their simple wisdom helping me to clear my heart centre.

Everything we give out to plants, rocks, minerals or any form of nature is returned to us. We should never underestimate the power of nature. The colour of nature is green, which is the colour of the heart centre.

FIFTEEN

Balance

As a car driver I like to keep my car clean, have it serviced regularly, check the oil and tyre pressure and make sure I have enough petrol.

Then I can relax and feel I have done everything possible to ensure safe, smooth journeys.

Our journey through life will run more smoothly and comfortably if we check the different parts of ourselves.

If we drive our car with one of the tyres over or under inflated, then the whole car is out of balance. It is up to the driver to check the tyres. Would you drive with one rock hard tyre and the others soft? Or would you bump along on a soft tyre? Probably not.

The four tyres represent the four aspects of our being – mental, physical, spiritual and emotional. Most of us journey through life with them out of balance.

If we are physically fit and yet we block off all our emotions, we are out of balance. Our physical tyre is just right and our emotional one flat.

If we sublimate everything to prevent ourselves experiencing pain and hurt, our spiritual tyre is over-inflated and our emotional one low. Or we may sublimate everything and not think things through, so that our mental tyre is low.

The person who is all in his head, the thinker, the intellectualiser, often runs with his mental tyre rock hard to the cost of the other three.

Very materialistic people commonly have a flat spiritual tyre.

It is worth looking at ourselves and trying to imagine how balanced the four aspects of our being are. We can ask ourselves if we are in balance or if we are going crabwise or lopsidedly or bumpily. It is obviously so much easier and more enjoyable to travel through life in balance.

Keith came to see me looking as if he was about to burst. He was overweight and drank and smoked too much. Inside he was a pressure cooker of repressed anger and hurt.

He spent long hours at work, thinking, calculating and intellectualising. Because his life had been spent amassing money, he had no time to enjoy nature or appreciate the finer aspects of life.

Using the analogy of four tyres, Keith's physical and spiritual tyres were flat and the mental and emotional ones hard. No wonder he was having problems running his life.

He was using cigarettes and drink to keep his emotions down. He cut down on both and started to give vent to his feelings during our sessions. I could almost feel air hissing out of the emotional tyre as he reduced the pressure.

He started walking each morning to the station and in a park during his lunch hour. He began to get physically fitter. And as we discussed the Spiritual Laws of the Universe, he opened to the inner knowledge he already had and looked at the higher aspects of life with new interest.

As he began to balance out, he felt much more comfortable about his life. His weight dropped and he was able to give up smoking, which was only an outward manifestations of how he felt inside.

When our car tyres are unbalanced, we feel out of control. If you feel unsafe and out of control in your life, check the balance of your mental, physical, emotional and spiritual aspects.

One of the most important lessons of life is learning to balance the masculine and feminine energies. Power is a masculine energy, while wisdom is a feminine one and power without wisdom is dangerous indeed. It is like letting a child drive a fast car.

We all have power, which we can use for good or to make people afraid. We can use power to repress our children, to impose our will on people, to force people to do things for us, or to control our relationships.

Blackmail is a fear that unless we use the power of threat, we won't be able to get what we want. Most people are aghast at blackmailers and feel anger and rage against them. Then they go home and emotionally blackmail those close to them. There is no difference.

I can look back at times when I've bribed or black-mailed my children. 'If you don't do what I tell you I'll use my power against you.' What I actually threatened was that if they didn't do what I wanted, I'd smack them or not give them any sweets until they'd apologised, or send them to their room.

I was not listening to my inner wisdom. It is wasteful for me to feel guilty or judgemental against myself. I must accept that's where I was then, and undoubtedly often still am, and trust that through acceptance, my wisdom can grow.

Most of us only have the opportunity to be potentates in our own little world. We can think of people like Hitler or Stalin, who have used their power against mankind, without the balance of wisdom. They are doing on a large scale what many of us do on a small one.

When wisdom and power are in balance we live in harmony with ourselves and other people.

Masculine energies are the thinking, intellectual, doing, thrusting, seeking elements of our natures, and of course they are very necessary for us to grow and accomplish. Feminine energies are the healing, intuitive, creative, wise, accepting, being elements.

When the masculine and feminine energies within an individual are balanced, then that person is whole.

We in the West live in a masculine dominated culture, where emphasis is placed on doing. When children sit quietly, they are told to 'do' something. A client told me that she was woken every morning as a child by her father shouting, 'Time to get up and do'.

Many people feel guilt ridden when they sit down

during the day. They may even have to become ill to give themselves permission to rest. They have to justify their existence by doing something. They are conditioned to be masculine dominated.

In our masculine orientated culture, success is measured in terms of how well we are doing, either materially or in exams or promotion.

And of course, people can go out with energy in a thrusting, dominating, forceful way to acquire possessions, status and certificates to say they have succeeded.

However, all the doing and getting in the world, won't help us to be at peace, because we fear material things can be taken away from us if we stop doing.

All the degrees on the wall to show we've succeeded won't guarantee success without the wisdom and intuition to apply the knowledge.

Knowledge can be acquired by our masculine aspect but the wisdom to use it must come from the feminine, receptive, inner voice within us.

The Eastern culture is influenced by the feminine. There we have an acceptance of mysticism and spirituality, but lack the balance of the masculine to do something, so people sit back and wait passively.

The East recognises the importance of the inner world and tends to undervalue the importance of the outer. We in the West value the outer and tend to ignore the inner.

When we are passive be-ers we find our life flows past us, so that we do not accomplish what we intended to accomplish when we made our life choices.

It is important to integrate the masculine and feminine within our personalities. This means listening to our inner voice, trusting our wisdom, contracting our spiritual being and having accepted the voice of wisdom, use the masculine energy to put that wisdom into effect.

The be-er conceives the vision. The do-er materialises it. Both aspects are necessary.

Because of the emphasis in our culture on doing we feel we are not valued unless we do something for others.

Susan was a typical example. She was a bespectacled, curly haired grandmother who spent much of her time trying to please her children by doing things for them.

She felt she had to bake them cakes or look after their dogs or babysit. One day she arrived for her session very upset because she couldn't babysit for her son when he asked her.

I asked whether her son was upset that she couldn't do it for him. She sounded quite bemused. 'Well, no actually. He didn't seem to mind at all.'

She was projecting all her need to 'do things for people' onto her children.

I asked if her children would be happy to see her without her doing anything for them. She paused to think.

'They'd probably prefer it', she admitted slowly.

What a realisation!

When we stop needing to do and let ourselves be, we can actually listen to people. We can be there for them. We can be at home for ourselves.

If we can be there for someone, we can hear what their needs are and do what they want, not what we think they need.

When we balance the doing and being in our lives, we are performing with wisdom. We sense the need and then use energy to do something about it.

We relax and allow creative ideas to flow. Then we gear ourselves into action to put the ideas into reality.

When the wisdom and spirituality of the East integrates with the power and energy of the West, then the world will be in harmony. As each of us individually starts to balance our masculine and feminine aspects, this spreads into the collective, speeding up world harmony.

It is not by chance that we are called human beings, not human doings. We talk of angelic beings, or beings of light.

The work each of us does in understanding and balancing ourselves, is an offering to the Universe.

The left side of the brain deals with the intellectual, thinking, rational, reasoning, calculating, masculine side of our natures.

In our education system, this side is developed almost to the exclusion of the right brain.

The right side deals with the wise, creative, receptive, intuitive aspect. When we develop this side of the brain equally with the left, then we will indeed produce super children – whole people.

When the right and left, or masculine feminine, yin yang are balanced, we have people who listen to their bodies and act on what they hear, artists who conceive ideas and have the energy to manifest their conception, groups who visualise a peaceful, harmonious community and have the determination and strength to make it happen, wise leaders who have vision and the strength to put it into effect.

In the West we learn to undervalue and block off our right brain function. Yet we all have wonderful gifts of creativity, intuition and the ability to sense the unseen energies of the Universe. To the extent that we block off these gifts we are denying God within us.

Children who see auras, talk to angels or fairies, have an invisible playmate, or see ghosts, are told not to be stupid. We tell them they are imagining things. So we deny God to our children. Because of us they deny some of the wonders of the Universe.

There are seven main energy centres in the body. They look like flowers or discs of whirling energy and are known as chakras. The top one is at the crown of the head and is violet, the third eye in the centre of the forehead is indigo, the throat is blue, the heart centre is green, the solar plexus yellow, the abdomen orange and the base centre is red.

If our energy is mainly working in the bottom three chakras, then we may be violent, emotional, sexual, frightened or very practical.

If we raise our consciousness to the top three chakras, we can be ungrounded and unworldly. If we are up in the air all the time we are not earthed and we are on the planet earth for an earth experience.

Many spiritual people stay in the top centres. They are

usually very holy and spiritual and loving. And they ignore and deny the suppressed emotions which clog the lower chakras. They are not balanced people.

Energy needs to run freely through all our centres. Until we can live in the heart, centred and balanced, we are not whole.

To be centred we must accept and release the sexual and emotional blocks, express and release the hurts and angers. At the same time we need to understand why we've drawn our hurtful or upsetting experiences and how we've created our blocks. Accepting and acknowledging, helps us to learn our lessons. Then spiritual energy really can flow freely through us.

I understand that certain very old souls have made a karmic choice to work only on the spiritual levels. They have already cleared their blocks and can use their lives to send light to mankind.

So many of the lessons of life are to do with balance.

Most of us have lessons to learn concerning money. We may need to learn the balance between being greedy or undervaluing ourselves or between hoarding and blithely spending.

There is a balance between seriousness and fun, work and play, giving and receiving in all areas of life.

We are here to work on ourselves and must get this in balance with serving others.

We are learning to love ourselves and others unconditionally. While we learn this we have to balance getting our needs met and offering love to others.

When we use common sense we are balanced.

SIXTEEN

The Body is a Reflection of the Mind

Have you ever felt tired and dispirited, with a headache or tummyache and then someone has come up with a bright idea or an exciting invitation or interesting news? The headache, and tummyache vanish. The tiredness is replaced by energy. And the only thing that has changed is your state of mind. Your body merely reflected it.

It is the same with all illness, pain and depression. The body is a wonderful instrument to tell us what is going on in our mind.

We can lie to ourselves about our feelings and emotions but our body never lies.

If someone says they want to do something and their eyes shift away, their body is saying otherwise. If we say we are comfortable about something and cross our arms, our body says we are not comfortable about it. If we then retort that we always cross our arms because we feel more comfortable that way, then we so habitually feel threatened, that it is indeed the only position we feel comfortable in.

Ills in the body are a way of indicating to us that something is not well in our psyche. By definition all dis-ease indicates that we have violated a spiritual law, and so for every physical manifestation, there is a metaphysical equivalent.

When we heal the mental, emotional and spiritual blocks, then the physical problems heal.

So many of us want the world to see our nice, charming, generous aspects that we manfully, uncomplaining shoulder the burdens. Smiling we do the donkey work, while others relax. We bury inside the hurt, resentment, anger or bitterness and often deny those feelings even to ourselves, but the feelings are held in our bodies and show as cancer or arthritis or heart conditions or some other physical condition.

Our thoughts are more powerful than our words because we can lie with our tongues. Our thoughts affect our bodies and manifest as ill health.

The old saying went, 'Sound in mind, sound in body.'

The channels of our bodies are like rivers. If a river is sparkling clear and smooth flowing, the banks remain intact and graced with grass and flowers. It is beautiful and harmonious. When we hold clear beautiful thoughts, the channels of our body are clear. We are healthy.

If we churn up the mud with resentment and criticism, the silt settles on the bends and forms mud banks. In arthritis the inharmonious emotions change the chemical composition of the blood and the silt forms deposits in the joints.

With anger the river becomes a torrent. We can feel our pulse pounding when we are really angry. If the torrent continues long enough it will overflow the banks at a weak point and create a flood. In the same way if we nurse hurts and grievances, we will make growths, or erode the banks and form ulcers, or weaken the banks to allow in viruses and infections.

We are constantly surrounded by viruses and germs and the bodies of every healthy person naturally contains cancer cells. They can only flourish and develop if we create the right environment for them.

Fear creates tension which constricts or blocks the flow in the body, allowing disease or illness to flourish.

In a smoothly flowing harmonious river, no weeds can take hold to clog it, no mud churns, no torrents rage, no whirlpools eat away at it. Generous, kind, joyous, prosperous, loving thoughts open up our hearts and all the channels of our body. A rich full blood supply flows to every part of our body. No illness or virus can take root and flourish. They sweep through and leave us unaffected.

People sometimes deny the connection of the mind and the body. Yet if we receive a shock we faint. If we feel belittled we get a headache. If we are upset we feel sick. There is always a connection.

We watch a fearful scene on TV and find our stomachs tightening. We are reacting physically for an instant or two to the pictures we are seeing. If we constantly clench our stomachs we will give ourselves ulcers or appendicitis or let some disease into that area.

If we want to argue or speak up for ourselves and cannot or dare not, our throat will tighten. The more often we hold our throat in tension, the more likely we are to give ourselves laryngitis, tonsilitis or some other throat ailment.

Maybe our chest contracts every time we feel hurt or rejected. If we are constantly feeling hurt and are therefore constantly tensing our hearts, we will give ourselves angina or heart problems. Releasing and forgiving opens our heart physically and spiritually.

Love expresses as total health. So we can only be ill where we hold a negativity. Every part of our body tells us something about what is going on at a deeper level within us.

The right side of the body directly reflects our feelings about the men in our life, fathers, brothers, husbands and male friends. It also relates to our work or careers and to our masculine aspect.

The left side of the body relates to the women in our life – mothers, sisters, female friends and to the healing, caring aspects of our characters and to our feminine aspect.

A client's husband had just left her. She was full of anger towards him. She didn't know what way to go in life now that he had gone. The ankle represents our direction in life. Her emotions were directed at a man, so it was inevitable she should hurt that part of her body. She tripped and broke her right ankle.

A family I know learnt that their mother was dying. Soon afterwards one of the sons was involved in an explosion and fire. He burnt only the left side of his body. He was 'exploding' with rage inside at his mother for leaving him.

A few days later his brother broke his left arm. Our arms represent the way we embrace life and the younger boy felt broken inside about embracing life without his mother.

One sunny day I found myself sitting on a bench next to a teenage lad. He was nursing his right knee while he watched his friends playing sport. He told me that he couldn't do games any more because his knee always played up.

I suggested as gently as possible that if he could be a little more flexible about what his father wanted him to do about his career, it would get better.

He looked at me as if I was a witch and said, 'How do you know?' The knees are to do with the ego. Joints are concerned with flexibility and change. His knee was locked. The right side is the father principle and career. So his body was showing the world what was going on in his mind.

He told me that he and his father were locked in a battle because he wanted to be an artist and his father wanted him to go to university and become a banker. His inner conflict was expressed in his body.

Our spines support us. If we do not feel safe about life or money or if we do not feel supported by a relationship, it can reflect in back problems. We can ask ourselves, 'Is someone on my back?' or 'Who is stabbing me in the back,' or 'Who isn't being supportive?' We can even ask, 'Am I not supporting myself and therefore feeling sorry for myself?'

A rich businessman I knew with no money worries was plagued with low back problems. He had spent all his life making money and said he never ever worried about money as he knew he could always make more. His body said otherwise but he didn't want to believe that.

Some time later he told me that his early memories

were of lying in bed listening while his parents discussed their money worries. Deep inside he held the fear of lack of money and spent his whole life making sure that he was financially safe. But the fear that it could all be taken away from him was locked into his lower back and kept it in tension.

The way we carry our shoulders indicates the way we carry ourselves through life. Are we bent under the burden of the problems we carry? Or do we walk tall?

When we get neck ache, we can ask ourselves, if someone is being a pain in the neck. Or are we being stiff necked about something or rigid in our thinking? Are we resisting someone or something?

The skin is a strong reflector of emotions. When we feel irritated it will itch. Who do we want to scratch? When we burn or boil with rage, it will erupt with spots or boils or become inflamed.

A client's relationship with his wife was fraught and difficult. He had burning sensations all over his body. He itched all over and felt he was going to burst. No amount of creams or medicines helped to ease the irritation.

But when he vocalised his rage about what was going on in his life in the safety of therapy sessions, the burning and itching ceased.

Our eyes represent the way we see things in life. If we are afraid to look at things in our lives we tense up our eye-balls and become short sighted. Eye problems indicate that we don't like what we see in our lives, or that we are afraid of what we see. Many students are bored by the thought of the years of study that they see ahead. No wonder so many need glasses.

Years ago when I was an expatriate wife, I used to bring my children to England to boarding school each September. Each year I had a hayfever reaction which made my eyes burn and itch.

One September coincided with a particularly difficult emotional time in my life. When I came to England my eyes became inflamed and swelled up so badly that I couldn't see. Poor me, I thought. My allergy is getting worse.

Soon after this I started to take responsibility for what was happening in my life and gradually sorted out the emotional problems.

My children continued to go to boarding school each September but I didn't need to respond with inflamed itchy swollen eyes and thick head. The allergy disappeared.

My body had merely been showing me that I was angry and confused at what I was seeing in my life. I was burying the emotion but it emerged as an allergy.

We all selectively hear, based on our belief system. So if we expect to be hurt and rejected, we will pick out words and imbue them with the hurt or rejection we expect. If we expect to fail, we will read failure into what we hear.

We are tuned in to hearing what is important to us. This is why we selectively hear our name mentioned in a crowded room.

If we think we are beautiful, we will hear complimentary statements. If we think we are sexy and no one values us for anything else, we will selectively hear the comments about our sexiness.

When people say, 'You twisted my words', it means that you heard what you programmed yourself to hear and tailored the words to fit your belief system.

If we give ourselves earache we know that we don't like what we hear.

People with nagging or very talkative partners sometimes withdraw into deafness.

When we have constant vague fears and hurts we protect the channels of our bodies with walls. And so we harden our arteries.

More deeply held fears are buried more deeply within our bodies. So if we bury the fears and bad feelings in our livers or kidneys or gall bladder or bladders we need to look deeper within.

Know thyself and the Kingdom of heaven is thine. Our bodies are clues on the route.

Of course our bodily health is also affected by physical things. To be healthy we need to eat the right foods, take enough exercise, live in peaceful surroundings with enough stimulation and interest to keep us alert.

And when our minds are clear, joyous and in tune with our bodies, we automatically choose what is best for us mentally, physically, spiritually and emotionally.

A carthorse plods solidly through life whereas a delicate highly strung racehorse reacts to fears and impressions, to change, to different food and water. He responds to atmospheres and individuals and he is more physically delicate than the carthorse.

And we are no different. Some can plough their way unawares, unresponsive, unthinking through life.

Others are more sensitive. And the more sensitive we are, the more quickly our bodies will reflect our thoughts and feelings. So the uncleared guilt emerges as pain, the suppressed anger as constant infections.

We may feel exasperated that we are suffering from one thing after another because we can't get away with negative thoughts in the same way as someone else.

Those with more advanced consciousness who find emotions instantly mirrored in their bodily health are being given more opportunities to clear the inner levels and grow.

Ill health is also a test.

Some people choose to fight their main battles in the arena of their bodies. They naturally are more likely to become ill. Others choose other areas of their life for their main experience.

The more sensitive we become, the more open we are to other people's feelings and emotions and the more likely we are to pick up another's pain and illness. We need to strengthen ourselves.

When we radiate only love and goodwill, nothing and no one can come in to harm us or to take our energy.

However, while we work to reach that advanced level of love consciousness, we may need to visualise a protection.

A quick and effective protection is to cover yourself totally in a blue cloak. It is very effective simply to surround yourself with white light and ask for protection.

When we release our fears and illusions, we cannot be

ill. However on our journey we may need the help of drugs and medicines.

I've often heard people say that we should never take drugs as they merely alleviate the symptoms and never clear the cause, which lies within ourselves, thus they prevent us from growing and developing.

There is some truth in this but I believe that everything is God given and therefore drugs do have a place. Certainly if we use drugs as a substitute for looking within, we are misusing them. We can recognise they alleviate symptoms to give us time and strength to locate the inner source of our problem.

It is very difficult to look honestly within for the inner source, while we are in a fever or racked with pain. When drugs help us to overcome a life threatening disease, we are given an opportunity within the same life to look for the reason why we created the disease in our body. Nothing is wasted. Nothing is by chance.

Our emotions create our body size and shape. Tall thin people suppress their feelings and grow upwards to get away from them. They are often gentle and non-assertive (and angry inside).

I read an article recently in which many mothers reported that their children stopped growing for a year after their father died. Their emotions affected the growth of their bodies.

Our bodies show where we are emotionally stuck. Some of us have large intellectual heads and small bodies. Our intellect has grown and our emotions remained in childhood.

Women who block off their sexuality in their teens remain small busted. Women who are over nurturing develop large busts.

I saw a businessman take off his smart suit jacket and jump up and down. Without the jacket, it was clear, he had the chest and body development of a seven year old. His emotional response to life was that of a seven year old and he was a successful business man despite that. How much more successful could he have been with emotional maturity.

Fat is fear. When we feel unsafe, some of us put on weight to protect our vulnerable inner selves.

Some fat is flabby and watery and full of unshed tears and hurts. Others form solid tight fat which is a rigid armouring to protect the inner being.

If we feel we need to be big and strong, we will put the fat on our shoulders. If we feel emotionally vulnerable we will put it on our tummy for we hold our emotions in our abdomen. When we hold onto our childhood hurts and emotions we retain fat on our hips and thighs.

Before birth we choose our bodies and then we shape them during our life with our emotions.

SEVENTEEN

Soul Choices

Our soul is the sum total of our lives and experiences. It is like a diamond and in each life we choose a facet of our diamond to work on. If the work on one facet is not completed in one lifetime then we undertake it in another.

So what we do and think, how we react to people and how much we put into life, affects not only what happens to us in the near future but also what happens to us in the far future.

Before we are conceived our Higher Self chooses what we are going to work on during our lifetime. We choose the lessons we want to learn, the experiences we need to undergo and the fears we need to face. These are pre-programmed within us.

And in order to attract the experiences we need we then decide on our parents, our family, our body, our sex, our nationality, our country and date of birth.

Not a single thing happens by chance. Those difficult people and situations are there for a purpose.

Our glandular system, our genetic inheritance, family predispositions, the culture we are born into are choices.

A soul may choose very difficult life circumstances, say poverty, cruelty, early abandonment or a weak mind because he wants the opportunity to clear a lot of karma in one life. Or he may want to choose a difficult test for his soul so that he can develop faster. His growth depends on how he handles those circumstances so it depends on whether he responds to what is thrown at him with bitterness and hate or with love and acceptance.

And of course we can continue to choose easy lives but

most people don't want to spend their years walking in the foothills of life. They want to advance to climb the mountain.

So we choose our particular parents because, with their beliefs and fears, they will offer us the perfect opportunity to attract the lessons and experiences we need.

In the womb the baby receives physical and emotional nourishment from its mother. Any fears which she holds, automatically block off this nourishment and so affect the baby emotionally as well as physically.

In extreme cases where the mother has undergone an emotional trauma, the baby has miscarried because her body is no longer a welcome vehicle.

Emotion is not a one way communication. The baby has come from Light into its confinement in the womb and sometimes feels very angry and afraid. When we are in the Light and making free choices from a point where we can see all the possibilities, it is easy to see how much we can accomplish. In the womb the memory of the Light fades until we are in the dark in every sense.

It is one thing to sit with experienced advisors on a clear bright day and look at a distant island out in the ocean. We study the chart with all the rocks and shallows and tides and are sure that we can make it.

However, the chart is taken away and we find we have to face those rocks and shallows and tides at night in pitch blackness. Maybe our boat is leaky or rudderless and the seas running high. We find our confidence ebbing and fear setting in. It is the same for the incoming soul on his journey.

So many of us make choices for our higher growth and development but we do not like what we choose.

Many mothers feel guilty if they are sick or unwell during pregnancy and feel they haven't done their best for the baby. Indeed it may be that emotional pressures on the mother have caused problems for the baby but it works the other way too.

The baby may be experiencing fear or frustration in the womb. Some souls may be feeling reluctant to return for another earth journey and make themselves ill with anger and fear. Naturally the mother picks up these feelings and can also become unwell.

When we choose our parents before our birth we know all there is to know about them. We know about their character, their strengths and weaknesses, as well as the pressures and influences they are under. We know how their mind works and what choices they will make. We know, therefore, if they are likely to abort us.

So to be aborted or to miscarry or to die at birth are often pre-choices. The incoming spirit may only have needed the experience of being in the womb, perhaps only needing to experience confinement.

A soul sometimes offers to enter that mother's body, however briefly, so that the mother and all concerned can undergo that particular experience.

Sometimes the reality of what we have chosen to experience in a lifetime seems too difficult when we actually have to face it. To come from light and awareness into gravity and ignorance is a formidable ordeal for many, and the soul needs much love and compassion.

Some cot deaths are early choices to give up, as are some miscarriages.

If the mother chooses to have an abortion and the incoming soul really needs to experience a life on earth at that time, it will select another vehicle and start again. If the incoming soul is very linked with that family and particularly needs a life experience with that family circle, it will wait for a more propitious time and come then.

We tend to be so judgemental about abortion. I believe there is no judgement, only learning.

I'll never forget talking to Maggie. She was a most beautiful, spiritually aware, elderly lady, with neatly swept back grey hair and a gentle, loving face. Many, many years ago she had had an abortion and had often wondered about it. One day she was sitting in her meditation circle and had entered a deep state of meditation. She saw her baby in another woman's arms. She saw the love for herself in the baby's eyes and knew that all was well. That soul had now chosen a different mother and was embarking on a new earth experience. The baby had linked in to let Maggie know and Maggie glowed with happiness and love as she related what she had been shown.

Children who die young are often old souls who choose a short life because they only want to undertake one particular experience and when it is done they go home. More commonly they offer to be born to give their family a learning experience. Handling the experience of a child dying is a major test and lesson for all concerned.

I have often heard that all children who die young have pre-chosen that span of years before birth. However I feel there are still choices.

One of my daughters had meningitis in babyhood and we were told by the doctors that she had become a deaf, blind vegetable and could not live until morning.

To the amazement of everyone she came out of a deep coma and made a complete recovery.

For years I thought guiltily, if only I'd done this or that maybe she wouldn't have been so ill. However when I left the victim role behind and started to look at the law of cause and effect and life choices, I learnt that she had chosen to come into this life with a deep fear to clear. This fear was recorded in her spine and when a cold virus came along it naturally fastened into the fear. Then it travelled to the brain and developed as meningitis. If there had been no fear the virus would have passed straight through without attaching to her.

I asked if I might be shown what happened for her in a past life and was shown her as a six year old in another life where she died of a similar virus. She gave up and did not fight for life. She did not learn her lessons in that life, so she did not clear her karma.

I believe that while she was so deeply unconscious, her spirit was in consultation with those higher beings who guide her and she decided to come back and go through with this life.

Babies and children can also become ill because of outside influences. They are open to the feelings of those around them and pick up those feelings.

Babies are so in tune with their mother's feelings that

they will react to anything their mother reacts to. The baby has many of its fears and beliefs pre-recorded and if the mother is reacting to a fear that the baby holds already, the baby will plug in and respond. This is why babies and small children seem to take on their mother's fears as their own.

Babies and children also react to the mother's expectations. If we expect our child to get a stomach bug like the other children at playschool, we plant the expectation in the child's mind which opens the way for it to enter. The more strongly we hold the expectation the more likely the child is to get the stomach bug.

In the same way, if we fear our child will do something we don't want him to do, we communicate that fear telepathically to him. If we hold that fear in our minds the child will be constantly picking up the thought of doing that undesirable thing and become open to doing it.

Have you heard a parent say to a child, 'Don't you dare cross that road on your own'. The child had no intention of crossing the road until the parent planted the idea. Thoughts are the same as words. We plant them.

Babies and children are extremely sensitive. The hardest thing for a child to maintain health and commonsense against is an over concerned mother.

All illnesses are tests. A soul may choose a genetic inheritance which has a pre-disposition towards some condition – asthma, cancer, arthritis for example. If we learn our lesson before the illness manifests, we won't get the illness. We won't need to. The disease will flow through us and leave us untouched. If we cannot do so, and often difficult learnings for our particular soul are involved, then we must undertake our karma and be tested and tried by the illness.,

One multiple sclerosis sufferer told me that she dreamt as a child she was turned into a stone statue. Even though she was quite young, she recalled the dream vividly and felt it was some kind of prophecy. The dream was indeed a warning to her. She ignored it. She became inflexible in her attitudes and rigid with fear of life. She hardened herself to the Universal Truths and she fulfilled the dream.

Another multiple sclerosis client heard the Truth. Like a tight closed bud exposed to sunlight, she opened up and accepted the Light. She literally saw and felt it come into her. She knew instantly that she had been totally miraculously cured. She threw away her walking stick and joined dancing classes to express her joy and thanks.

Mankind has individual as well as collective karma to work through on sexuality.

At an aware level most of us think sex is desirable and wholesome and at a deeper, often repressed level, we nearly all hold beliefs about sex being dirty and sinful.

Collectively mankind has held and passed on beliefs about sex being impure, shameful and imperfect. How many of us in thought or words have condemned another's sexual exploits or aberrations as being disgusting, depraved or not nice?

Whatever we condemn in another lies unacknowledged in ourselves and deep within most of us lies sexual guilt.

Most of us block off our sexuality to some extent through guilt and fear. So we block off God, by violating the Law of Acceptance or the Law of Non-Judgement.

The Truth is that we are light and pure. Every cell of our body is light and pure. God did not selectively make our sexual organs black or dirty. God is Love and Light. How could Love and Light create anything impure? Sexuality is pure and purity can never be tarnished. It is our false perception of sexuality which makes us think this.

I am not condoning lust and sexual aberrations and promiscuity. They all come from fear. When we let go of the fear and see the Truth, we no longer need to manifest the fear with lust and aberrations and promiscuity.

When we hold repressions and guilts about sex, fear meets fear during intercourse. A baby is conceived in fear.

When we believe that the male penis and female vagina are expressions of Love, then intercourse becomes a spiritual blending and if a baby is conceived, he is conceived in love.

Our bodies express our feelings about our sexuality. Confusion is expressed as swellings, and many women nowadays are expressing their confusion about their sexuality and their feminine role with pre-menstrual tension. Swollen breasts, tummies and fluid retention are commonplace. Guilt and uncertainty cause tension and pain.

It is small wonder that Aids and other sexually transmitted diseases are rampant. The viruses attach to sexual blocks and guilts.

Aids is a disease of self destruction, based on self hatred and we can only hate ourselves when we block out the Light within us. So many people now have lost sight of their inner Light that they are destroying themselves.

When, individually and collectively, we let go of our guilts and fears about sexuality, Aids can have no foothold. It will disappear.

Aids is knocking on the door of mankind to tell us it is time to accept our sexuality and release our sexual fears. Most of all it is telling us to find our inner Light and love ourselves.

EIGHTEEN

Images and Symbols

The medium for communicating with the inner mind is images and symbols. It is a two way process. We can put instructions into our computer and get information about our inner beliefs out.

Denise had had many anxieties and tricky relationships through her life, so I took her on an imagery journey to see how she handled her problems.

She saw herself striding along a country path, cheerfully enough, but as soon as she reached a fallen tree, she turned into a child and found herself scrambling, torn and bleeding, with great exertion over the barrier.

As soon as she was over the tree she grew up again and strode purposefully on until she reached a bramble patch. Once more she turned into a child and tore her way panic stricken through it. Throughout the inner journey, she became a child each time she met an obstacle.

When I asked her to pause in front of the obstacles and remain an adult, she could negotiate each one calmly and easily. As a result of the imagery she saw quite clearly that she met her life's problems from the level of the inner child.

We were then able to discuss ways that she could stand back and look at her problems so that she could handle them with adult perception and resources.

Stored in our minds we have a treasure house of resources that we often under utilise. Sometimes we never even open the doors available to us. As a result of her changed understanding, Denise became calmer and more objective about her problems. She was then able to access inner resources she never knew she possessed.

What had been mountains to the old Denise became molehills to the aware, adult Denise.

Maureen simply didn't know if she could save her marriage. She was in such a turmoil that nothing seemed clear.

On her inner journey down a river, she found that a huge tree had fallen across the river. This represented the state of her marriage in the river of her life. She tried to see if there were enough of the roots left in the bank to anchor the tree if it was lifted.

The confusion in her mind blotted out her ability to see clearly in her life and this was reflected in her inner journey.

First it was too misty to see the tree roots. I asked her to let the sun shine down to clear the mist. It cleared. Then there was an obstacle which blocked her vision. We moved it. She found she was still too far away to see the roots. However near she manoeuvred she couldn't see clearly enough.

We tried several more methods of seeing, until at last she imagined she was holding really powerful binoculars and clearly saw that there was enough root to save the tree.

She realised that she needed help to tackle the lifting. In her imagination she organised the help easily – and with that help she soon had the tree upright and firmly rooted again.

Her inner computer had revealed to her that with work and with help she could save her marriage.

Because she knew that it was possible to rescue her marriage, she was able to summon her courage and enthusiasm to start the necessary work.

Ken's relationship with his wife was uncomfortable and distant. He did not know what to do.

On an inner journey Ken saw that he and his wife were each walking down opposite sides of a busy road. Whenever there was an opportunity to cross neither did so because each hoped the other would make the first move.

He saw that one of them had to take the decision and as he was the only one with awareness, he crossed at the first possible chance. His wife greeted him with open arms and delight.

They walked hand in hand into beautiful peaceful meadows.

So many people literally do walk through life on the opposite side of the road from their partners. Fear of rejection or of losing power or control stop them from coming closer.

Ken's visualisation showed him that he must make a positive move towards his wife and that she would then respond. He decided to take an interest in her work instead of hoping she would be interested in his. Because he genuinely was interested in what she did, she responded by being much warmer and friendlier, so their journey into the peaceful meadows began.

Lucy came to me because she was overweight and felt that her life was chaotic. When I asked her to visualise herself as slim, she felt a pain in her head. I asked when she first experienced that pain and she saw herself as fourteen with her head being squashed with a weight, so that her eyes were squinting and her body deformed.

As she took the heavy weight from her head, her body became straight, her eyes straightened and she danced with joy. She put the weight on the floor and a porcupine emerged. I suggested she ask it what it represents. 'It's the pain', she said.

She wanted to stroke it and as she did so the bristles became softer and a whole row of crippled porcupines emerged. They each turned into people she knew, but crippled, deformed and distorted. I explained they were all perfect. Only her vision was distorted.

She opened her heart and accepted each person exactly as they were. As she did so they transformed into beautiful, whole smiling people. Lucy accepted that all the crippled people were parts of herself – and as she accepted herself exactly as she was, she would be healed.

Her headaches were the weight of her judgement on herself.

Everything we see in life we see from our point of inner perception. The reality is perfect.

*If we see anyone or anything as imperfect, the imperfection
lies within us. The Plan is perfect. Our comprehension is not.*

Martin said that his main problem was that he let his
paperwork pile up and get out of control. I asked him to
visualise what happened for him.

He saw himself drifting down a deep slow river and
soon came upon a pile of logs and debris which blocked
it. He tried all manner of ways to get round it but finally
realised that there was no alternative other than setting to
and clearing the jam.

Once he'd set about the task methodically, it cleared
quite quickly as log after log was released to float away.

'How stupid', he said when he opened his eyes. 'I knew
that anyway. I waste hours trying to avoid paperwork and
I have to do it in the end. It's the same with everything in
my life.'

We discussed how he could clear the log jams in his
life. He went home and sat at his desk and cleared his
paperwork. Then he methodically and honestly looked at
the many people who sponged on him. He took some firm
decisions. He examined the way he let people clutter his
life emotionally. He made some phone calls and cleared
his diary. He belonged to all kinds of societies and
organisations because he felt he ought to. He wrote letters
of resignation.

'It's a funny thing,' he said, when he next saw me. 'I
feel so much better and I haven't been constipated since.'

It's no wonder. He'd been giving symbolic messages to
himself about letting go on every level.

People who hoard things tend to be emotional hoarders
too, so they hold on and naturally their bodies respond by
holding on. So if you get constipated clear the junk from
your cupboards, your life and your body.

If our house is filthy, the windows dirty, every room a
mess and the garden overgrown, we are telling everyone
about our inner state of negativity and confusion.

If on the other hand we clean and tidy the house, weed
and beautify the garden and keep it that way, then our
mind clears and brightens.

There was a time when I would have a perfect front

garden. If I didn't have time for both, the back would be neglected. I needed to present a perfect front to the world, while the unseen parts of me were neglected. Now I am comfortable if there are a few weeds in sight. I don't have to put all my energy into appearing perfect. I am more willing to accept myself as I am. This gives me more time to cultivate my inner garden.

Our inner mind translates symbolic gestures and puts them to work. When I clean my windows I tell myself my vision is becoming clearer and I can see clearly my path ahead in life.

Kit complained that he really couldn't sort out the muddle in his life. He presented a coping facade to the world and inside he felt confused and chaotic.

I asked him to imagine himself in a garden and he found himself in a huge hillside garden without boundaries. It was covered in nettles and debris and brambles. In his imagination he worked very hard to clear it and created a beautiful pond in the contours of the hill.

When the garden was cleared and planted to his satisfaction he saw with dismay a horde of little bugs arrive and spread weeds and debris everywhere. When he asked them to leave, they told him it wasn't his garden and he wasn't entitled to a garden.

This was his belief in his own lack of value. At a deep level he didn't believe he was entitled to anything and shouldn't really be on earth at all.

I told him to stand tall and tell the bugs that the garden was his by Divine Right. As he did so the bugs turned and left without a murmur.

He had a moment of awareness that he was entitled to be in his garden in beauty and harmony. He knew then that he no longer had to justify his existence but could relax and harmonise his life. Every time he weeded his garden from that moment, he re-experienced and reinforced the truth.

How we relate to food symbolises how we allow ourselves to be nourished. Food represents emotional and spiritual as well as physical nourishment.

If we eat a resentfully prepared, poorly presented meal

while watching a violent film or arguing with the family, we are taking in resentment, anger, violence or distress. It is not surprising that so many people have digestion problems or emotional problems. They are not taking in nourishment with love. Acid emotions make for acid stomachs.

In a family where the food is prepared and cooked with love and care, the family absorbs the feelings. If they sit together in silence for a moment before they eat, their brain waves synchronise and harmonise, allowing the digestive juices to flow and the body, mind and spirit to prepare to receive nourishment.

If the meal is accompanied by happy conversation or good music, the nourishment is absorbed in peace and digested. The family is nourished in every way.

We need to watch not only what we eat but how we eat it.

Our minds contain all the wisdom and information we need to answer our life's dilemmas. When we learn to listen to our inner voice the answers can so often be presented to us. Sarah did not know what to do about her relationship. She felt that her boy friend had withdrawn.

I asked her to breathe deeply and relax and then visualise herself sitting under a tree in a meadow and see what happened. She relaxed immediately and soon saw her grandmother appear. The grandmother brought a mirror and held it up in front of Sarah. When Sarah looked into the mirror she saw herself and her boyfriend in wedding outfits.

'This is to be your inspiration when you doubt,' the old lady said. 'At the moment he needs your love and warmth but does not necessarily want it. He feels you are building your life around him and enclosing him. Find some interests of your own.'

Friends had given Sarah similar advice but she didn't hear it until her inner mind told her the same thing with such clarity.

Judith was happily married and a very capable career woman, who loved her job.

Her problem was that she couldn't decide whether or

not to start a family. She didn't want to jeopardise her career but she had to take a decision before she was too old.

I asked her to imagine she was on a hill, looking down on the pathway of her life. She followed it until it reached the present time where it forked.

She decided to set off along the right hand path. Ahead, perched on a hill, stood a glittering disneyland castle but the path to it led through dark trees and frightened her. I asked a wise lady to join her and they walked up to the castle together.

In front of the castle stood a white horse with a handsome prince sitting on it. Judith recognised the prince as her husband and saw herself there too standing alone and apart from him.

I suggested she looked inside the castle. She shivered when she looked inside. She said it was icy chill and piled high with gold.

She felt she wanted to leave and so she and the wise old lady returned down the path and took the left hand fork. This led past a beautiful waterfall to a cave. Inside it was spacious and yet was warm and comfortable.

Judith said, 'This old lady is showing me a picture of a baby. She says I can have it if I want it. It's my choice. And she's pointing out that the cave is nice and warm.'

Judith was very thoughtful when she opened her eyes. She knew she and her husband had much to discuss.

There are many times in our lives when we reach a fork and must make choices. When we look within we can help ourselves to make the right decision.

Judith wrote to me months later that as a result of our session they had decided to start a family and she was now pregnant. She added that she and her husband were so delighted, she couldn't imagine why they had agonised over the decision for so long.

Beauty is harmony. When we surround ourselves with beautiful objects, paintings, lovely gardens, we make a symbolic statement about our own beauty. And beautiful things harmonise our thoughts and lives.

Everything that is around us is symbolic of what is

going on inside us. Our car, our home, our garden, our animals, our friends are all reflecting parts of ourselves. Describe any one of them and we are describing some aspect of ourselves.

NINETEEN

Dreams

Dreams are messages about our lives. They may be warnings or advice or information about what we are really feeling at an inner level. They are always important and can short cut a tremendous lot of work on ourselves if we listen to them.

If you don't remember your dreams, then put a pad and pen by your bedside. Before you go to sleep impress upon your mind that it is to wake you when you have a dream. Repeat this instruction a number of times. Then tell yourself that you will remember the dream and go to sleep confidently expecting to do so. The moment you wake write down the dream before it slips away.

If you still can't remember your dreams it may be that you are too physically tired. Dietary factors can also interfere with dream memory, so check your diet.

When we want an answer about a problem we can ask for a dream to elucidate the situation or help with the problem. When we expect it to work, it does. It is generally accepted that every part of our dream is a part of ourself. So if we dream about Uncle Albert, then we should ask ourself what qualities we attribute to Uncle Albert. It may be that Uncle Albert is rigidly disapproving and the dream will be showing us something about that side of our character. Of course he may be jolly or generous or a courageous person so that in the dream he is that part of us.

I well remember when I was first coming into awarenesses about myself and I had a dream about someone I really disliked. I related the dream and then was asked what were the characteristics of this person I disliked so much. I judged him with relish. He was vicious, mean, unkind, avaricious and much more.

It was quite a shock to realise that I was describing a part of myself. I wanted to deny it as we all want to deny our shadow side but I had to take responsibility that there was an aspect of me which I was being shown.

We cannot deny a shadow is there any more than we can kick it to remove it or scrub it away. We must accept it and shine light on it. Then it disappears.

Dreams don't always mean what they appear to. A client had gone through a very bad time and had made really positive changes. She was looking very happy and bright.

As she left my room her face creased suddenly with a frown. She said, 'I just remembered that last night I dreamt my little girl died and I was pleased'.

I asked what characteristics she thought applied to her little girl at the moment and she replied promptly, 'Grumpy'.

'So the grumpy side of you has died and your dream mind just told you. No wonder you were pleased.'

She laughed and her frown cleared.

Of course it could have been a precognitive dream but then the feeling of the dream would have been totally different. People who have precognitive dreams usually know it.

We are often disturbed by dreams of death or of dead bodies. However the dream generally refers to some part of us that has died. Or it may refer to part of us that has been buried and needs to come to life now. Again if it is a warning, we will feel it in the dream.

I dreamed that two men were carrying a big burly man out of my house. The man was dead and they were taking the body away. It was just a snippet of a dream but I wanted to know more, so I went back into the dream and talked to the people in the dream. I discovered that the dead man was an aggressive bullying person and everyone was glad to see him go.

I had to recognise that part of me had been aggressive and bullying but that I didn't need that aspect of myself any more to protect me. Until then I must have needed the aggressive bullying part as a childhood survival strategy. My dream brought that element of my nature into awareness so that I could now release it.

Like dreams about death, dreams about funerals indicate the end of one state and the emergence into a new dimension. They can be very spiritual dreams. Who is being buried? And what are the characteristics of that person? Are you undergoing a transformation?

It is important to face fears which show up in dreams.

Moira was in the process of getting divorced. She kept dreaming that she went downstairs and found a hooded figure sitting in the dark. When she tried to turn the light on it wouldn't work. At this point she always ran away or woke up.

I always ask if someone can face a fear alone or if they need help. Sometimes a relative or friend will do. Sometimes it has to be a powerful, all protective figure like Christ.

Moira said she'd face the hooded figure alone. So she imagined herself back into the dream and walked downstairs into the sitting room. She turned the light on and because she was now directing the inner work, the light stayed on when she pressed the switch.

As she approached the hooded figure, he turned away to hide his face and each time she tried to see who it was, he managed to duck or avert his face.

Eventually she grabbed the hood and pulled it off. It was her husband, trying to frighten her into dropping the idea of a divorce. She talked to him and realised how fearful he was.

She also became consciously aware of the tactics he was using to frighten her out of suing for divorce. As she faced the fears and saw them for what they really were, she became stronger and more resolute, so that at last proceedings moved forward and were completed. She didn't need to have that dream again. Facing the fear had cleared it.

Pat kept dreaming that she was in a meadow, sitting under an oak tree, when a shadowy figure of a man would

come near her. She was always so terrified that she would
wake with her heart thumping.

She was quite fearful of facing this man in her inner
world but decided to do it alone. So she relaxed and saw
herself sitting in the meadow under the oak tree. When
the shadowy figure appeared, she asked him to come into
sight. It transpired that he was her dearly beloved grandfather who had died some years before and who wanted
to help her. He said he'd been trying to come close
enough to help her for a long time but she shut him out.

He often came to her in dreams after that and gave her
advice, comfort and help.

We may believe that it is the spirit of her grandfather
coming close to comfort her. Or we may believe that the
part of her which her grandfather represents, the wisdom,
the loving and caring part of herself, is giving this advice
and help. It does not matter. At the level where we are all
one, it is the same.

A bereaved person often dreams of the person who has
died. And this often brings great comfort. If we are not
open enough to sense the spirit of that person when we
are awake, it is often the only way they have of communicating with us – through our dream life.

I did some work with a man whose wife had died many
years before. He had nursed her through a terminal illness
and said he felt he had done all he could for her. I felt he
was still carrying guilt which was blocking his new
relationship.

He agreed to do a releasing exercise and realised that he
was indeed feeling very guilty that she had gone through
so much and he'd been so well. That night she appeared
to him in a dream and told him that she truly forgave him
and wished him well in his new relationship. He knew
then deep inside that he was freed.

When we don't complete the grief process after
bereavement or divorce or loss of any kind we can often
have our attention drawn to it by dreaming of that person
or those events. The feeling of the dream will then be
anything from sadness to total devastation and is an

indication to us that we have not healed the hurts at an inner level.

There are many books about the meaning of symbols in dreams. It is important that we are not too influenced by the book definition of a symbol. It is more accurate to sense what the object means for us.

People believe that certain items are phallic symbols and must be translated as such. Indeed they may be phallic symbols but if our computer has not recorded them as such they are not phallic symbols to us.

A client had a series of dreams about umbrellas, which are classic phallic symbols, but his umbrellas were colourful Mary Poppins umbrellas and the dreams were lovely spiritual messages.

We all respond to snakes in different ways. Some admire them, others loathe them. Some think they are crawling, lowly creatures and others think of them as transformation because they shed their skins. Some think of them as dangerous poisonous monsters and others as gently beautiful graceful forms.

So it is important to decide what a snake means for us if it appears in our dream. And that's how we translate it.

Dreams tell us about ourselves. If we dream about empty houses, we need to ask ourselves, are we empty inside? If the house of our dreams has extra rooms or hidden rooms, we are being told that there is more potential hidden within us than we realised. Each room we dream about symbolises something. Kitchens are where nourishment is prepared. Baths and showers are cleansing. We relax in a sitting room. Whatever we associate with a bedroom we are receiving a coded message about.

We may dream we are in the attic, which is the higher aspect of our consciousness or in the cellar, which represents the subconscious.

During dreams we may link with the wisdom of the Universe. Our personal mind computer has linked in with the Universal computer. We can link at a personal level as well as at a collective level.

We may receive information or advice for someone else or we may pick up a warning about an event or disaster somewhere else. Many people have dreamt of a friend or relative being ill or wanting help at the precise moment of their need.

When we have a precognitive dream we usually have a knowing that this is the case. We have linked into the Universal Intelligence, where time has no relevance. The same film can be showing in six cinemas in the town on one night and start at different times. We can see the middle in one before we see the beginning in another. Our dream has tapped into a future piece of life's film.

I was told of a lady who was expecting twins. A few days before the birth, she dreamt of a ship coming in to shore. As it docked, a radiant shining youth stepped ashore and helped a beautiful girl onto the land. Then the youth stepped aboard and, waving goodbye to the girl, sailed away.

When her twins were born, the girl lived and the boy died. But the mother knew that the boy had undertaken to conduct his sister to her start in life. He had fulfilled his mission.

June dreamt that she was in a crowd and an old man was holding her purse. She immediately assumed that he had stolen it and grabbed it back. He explained gently that he hadn't stolen it. He was holding it for her but she didn't believe him. However after she had thought about it she realised she was wrong, so she apologised to the old man.

Then a sexual relationship developed. She was a little defensive about the last statement so I asked what she felt about a sexual relationship. 'Oh, a beautiful bonding together and love', she said.

Her dream was to show her that her materialistic side and the wise spiritual side of her nature was bonding together in harmony.

Our dreams tell us what is really going on for us at that point in time.

I had an infection and was tossing in the night with the burning pain. I dreamt I was caught up in a coup in

Greece. I threw myself on the floor of the car and the rebels fired at the army over our heads. I knew I would be safe as long as I didn't see who the rebels were. I lay low and eventually escaped.

When I woke up and recalled the dream I was appalled. I'd been trying so hard to work out what the anger could be that let in the infection and my dream was telling me I was too scared to see.

I closed my eyes again and went back into the dream, picturing myself lying on the floor of the car. I knew that the army represented the authoritarian side of me that still holds me in control, demanding that I be strong and perfect and good. But who were the rebels?

There was no way I could see the rebels without being shot. It took time to manoeuvre myself into a position where I could see out safely.

There were the rebels – my teenage children, my partner and various clients who put high expectations on me!

At that time my teenage children were in the middle of the summer holidays and expecting me to do things with them. The man in my life expected me to do things with him. And one particular client expected me to wave a magic wand and make him better.

My dream told me that my fear of not living up to others' expectations was in conflict with the side of me that demanded that I be strong and perfect. No wonder the bit of me caught in the middle was so helpless and confused that I'd given myself an infection.

At this point of realisation one of my teenage daughters bounced into my room. I told her my dream and she laughed uproariously.

'I bet I was one of those rebels,' she said, omniscient as ever. 'I've been giving you a really hard time recently. You go back into your dream and negotiate a peace treaty, while I make you a cup of tea!'

I did negotiate a peace treaty both in my dream and in aspects of my life, thanks to the dream.

If we won't listen to our body's needs, it will try to get the message through to us somehow. Many nightmares are simply our body telling us we are eating the wrong foods.

Martin suffered from tummy aches, bladder tension and cystitis. He'd been treated many times with antibiotics which destroyed the healthy fauna of his intestines. I felt certain that he was suffering from candida, a yeast infection, which normally is kept in check in a healthy intestinal tract. Candida thrives on sugars and anything containing yeast. When it grows out of control, it creates problems and often a lot of pain in our bladders, intestines and sexual areas.

I had made suggestions to Martin about his diet, which he had half heartedly put into practice. Then he had lapsed and had been drinking alcohol and eating biscuits and cheese, all of which are food for the yeast infection and allow it to run riot.

When he came to see me had had a pain deep in his bladder for two days and was certain it would develop into a nasty cystitis attack.

That morning he felt his dream slip away as he woke. Left in his mind were the words, 'Beware of yeast'. The words were so clear that he sat up in bed in shock.

He believed what he was told and went immediately into a de-toxification programme, cutting out all the foods candida proliferates on. The pain was gone in two days and the cystitis didn't develop.

There are times when we appear to have no dream but an imprint is left in our consciousness. These imprints or messages are very important and should be heeded.

I have from time to time woken, or come out of meditation, feeling that I was being escorted back from a journey and the door was being closed on the journey. I remember nothing, but the message I come out with is always very important.

We store information in our mind computer in symbols. From the moment our soul began we have recorded our progress day by day. These records are kept by means of symbols and are stored in the third eye. These records are known as the akashic record and when we reach a certain level of progress we have access to our records.

According to Edgar Cayce some of our dreams are imprinted into our akashic record. The symbols in the dreams are used as a way to make a record of our soul's progress.

By looking honestly at our dreams, by interpreting the messages about our lower nature and doing something about it, we accelerate our growth.

Here are some instructions to help in this work.

1. Write the dream down and note the feelings.

2. Underline or extract the people and things in the dream and then describe them in the first person, as if you were that object or person. Each aspect of the dream is describing an aspect of you, eg, if you dream about a lion, a monkey and a tree, become the lion and describe yourself, your feelings and needs in the dream. Then take the monkey and the tree and do the same thing. You now have three aspects of yourself. How do they interact? What do they want to say to each other? What do they need from each other?

3. Imagine yourself back in the dream and give the people and things in the dream what they need. For example, if you dream that a flower is withered because it is getting no sunshine, go into the dream and plant it in the sunshine and watch it brighten and strengthen and open up. This gives your inner mind a symbolic message that the stultified part of you is ready to open up.

4. Do something or make a change that day in your life which confirms the new message to your inner mind.

TWENTY

Releasing Negative Ties

Whenever we send a thought to someone, we send a little energy impulse which forms a cord between us. If it is a casual acquaintance, the cord will be so fragile that it will fade away and disappear.

Parents and children, quite naturally, form strong cords which link them and which can be seen by those with clairvoyant sight.

When a child reaches adolescence he needs to be released from these reins in order to become an adult, who is free and responsible for himself.

All primitive societies recognise this and carry out a symbolic ceremony to release the adolescent to adulthood. However, in our culture, we don't do this – and because of this children often remain unhealthily influenced by parental attachments.

It is a restriction on an adult to be pulled and tugged by a parent. We wouldn't dream of putting harness and reins on a grown person. Yet there are many people who are emotionally manipulated by their parents without realising it.

These ties need to be cut so that the individual is free to become whole and independent in order that he can be emotionally free and responsible for himself.

Barbara told me that she and her son had a deteriorating relationship. She rarely saw him and although he was a man in his thirties and had a girl friend, he had never married.

I suspected that the cords had never been untied between mother and son, so that he was 'married' to his mother and therefore not free to marry anyone else.

Barbara understood immediately when I explained about uncording and was eager to perform the symbolic ceremony.

The day after we cut the cords between them, her son phoned her to say that he'd unexpectedly popped the question the night before. He was delighted with himself and couldn't understand why he hadn't taken the plunge before. Little did he realise he wasn't free to get engaged before because he was attached to his mother.

Many a person goes through a wedding ceremony when they are in fact still wedded to their mother or father and it makes their partner's task very difficult.

Like all symbolic ceremonies the purpose is to give a message to the inner mind. Phyllis Krystal in her excellent book, *Cutting the Ties that Bind*, describes how she takes her clients through a releasing, forgiving and healing ceremony so that the unconscious programming is powerfully changed.

She explains that when we are involved with someone we project part of ourselves onto them and they onto us, so we need to draw back into our own space before we do the cord cutting. She asks her clients to visualise themselves sitting in a circle. The person from whom they are being untied sits in another circle opposite. They then visualise light flowing round the two circles in a figure-of-eight.

The more vividly and frequently this exercise is done before the cutting, the more deeply the message enters our inner mind that we wish to be ourselves, no longer influenced by the other.

Nancy hated her mother. She constantly complained about her. According to Nancy her mother was a bitchy, critical, complaining old woman. Nancy, who was a mother herself, in her forties, spent a considerable amount of energy in spitting venom about her.

The record she churned out ran something like this, 'She expects me to phone her every week and she never phones me. She ignores the children or spoils them. She's always putting me down. After I've talked to her on the phone I feel sick. I feel so awful after I stay there for a weekend that I have to spend a day in bed' . . . and so on endlessly.

This dreadful harridan of a mother could do nothing right. It was a decidedly unhealthy relationship.

I explained about uncording and she was terrified it might alter their relationship! I told her that it had to be her decision and didn't hear from her for some weeks.

Then she phoned and said she'd been doing the figure-of-eight visualisation and decided that she would have to go through with it! It was as though she thought I was a dentist about to drill a tooth. Still terrified and seeking excuses she at last came for her session.

Indeed the cords she saw were big and black and like spider's tentacles. I asked her to cut them with a pair of golden spiritual scissors and she felt very relieved when they were finally removed. When the last one fell away she could at last see her mother as a lonely woman and could easily forgive her for the way she had behaved towards her.

Then she imagined herself turning and running into the sea and swimming until she felt cleansed and released.

A few days after the session her mother phoned and was very pleasant to her. It was the first time in many years that her mother had taken the initiative. She invited Nancy to stay for a few days.

Nancy visited her with love and a new understanding. The stay was beyond her wildest expectations. The relationship was now free to mature and develop.

When a parent and offspring have a bad relationship, they are invariably negatively corded.

My relationship with my father was strained for many years. When I decided to get myself uncorded from him, I could immediately see why we had problems.

A thick rope ran from his throat, looped round my neck and into my throat. Needless to say communication had been virtually impossible because I felt strangled.

I was shaken by the huge umbilical cord which ran from his third eye to my naval. For years I had a recurring dream that he was watching me having sex. In a physic sense he was. That dream never recurred after the cutting.

There were thin wires between our third eyes and our solar plexus. After the cords had been cut, removed and burnt on a bonfire, I felt light and liberated, with a conviction it was long overdue.

My mind had received a powerful message that I was now released to talk freely to my father. Because I was no longer being watched over I could be myself.

The following week he phoned me and for the first time ever I dared to express my feelings on many subjects. I said all the things that I had been strangling back for years. He had no idea how I'd been feeling and was appalled. Many of the misunderstandings, misrepresentations and bad feelings were cleared. It was a great moment.

Of course both negative and positive cords can reform if we continue to send the same thoughts towards someone, so it is up to us to keep ourselves free of the negative cordings.

Sasha was a beautiful but delicate woman, mother of two teenagers. She was frequently unwell. She had constant stomach problems and a listless tired feeling.

She was very sensitive to feelings and atmospheres and was certain that her mother was draining her.

When she visualised the cords she saw an iron bar between her chest and her mother's. It took some time to cut it with a hacksaw and pull the ends from the chest. As she removed the ends from her chest, the pains disappeared and she felt more alive. She saw herself throw her arms round her mother and thank her for all she'd done for her. Then she had the courage to tell her that now she wanted to be herself. She could see that her mother was reluctant to let her go but at last accepted it. Then Sasha threw the iron bar into a furnace and all her old clothes with it. They represented the old ways between her and her mother and she threw each item in with relish.

At last she cleansed herself in a shimmering silver fountain and put on elegant white trousers and top.

After the session Sasha's mother became unwell with chest pains and a feeling of lassitude. It isn't really surprising, because she had been living on her daughter's energy and needed time to adjust to living on her own energy. Within a few weeks her mother stabilised and Sasha reported that her parents' relationship with each other had improved considerably.

Now that she was no longer depending on her daughter, her mother was seeking to balance out with her husband. I have several times heard people say that after I uncorded them from one of their parents, the parents became closer to each other, often after an initial illness.

Vince was a very self-sufficient businessman. He had divorced some years ago after a short unsatisfactory marriage and was now a confirmed bachelor.

He had taken plenty of knocks during his life and had fought determindedly, yet somehow never quite achieving what he wanted to do. This feeling of never quite getting things right was familiar from childhood.

Vince came to me to seek help because he was always ill. He feared for his job if this continued.

His mother was demanding and querulous and Vince felt a good deal of frustration about her. He felt angry when he visited her and guilty when he didn't.

When he visualised his mother sitting in front of him and looked for the cords between them, he could clearly see a whole mass of them. He released them with determination but when it came to letting her go, he saw himself turn into a little boy and started to cry piteously, 'Don't leave me'.

It was not until his mother had left the inner scene that Vince was able to grow up.

He saw that his mother had never given him the caring and encouragement he needed nor had she freed him to become himself. He now became aware of the ambivalent relationship he had had with his mother and how he was constantly being tugged back to her apron strings, resenting it and yet not having the freedom and confidence to break away.

With the release of the psychic bonding he became able to visit her without resentment and choose not to visit her without feeling guilty. It was a big step forward in his growth.

Some parents put such deep controlling cords into their children that it is no easy matter to release them. Vicky had received such powerful messages about the evils of sex and the curse of being a woman from her mother, that it was surprising she had ever married or had a family of her own.

She had absorbed her mother's sexual anger and guilt at a very deep level. It caused severe problems with her health and her relationships.

When she looked for the cords they were so big and so deeply embedded into her sexual and abdominal areas that she could only visualise them being cut out under anaesthetic. She saw blood flowing copiously and she cried out with pain.

Because she was so incredibly sensitive Vicky felt terrible for a few days after this experience, sore and vulnerable, as if she had indeed had an earthly operation, but when she recovered, she found new health and strength – and a new relationship with her mother and her husband.

Couples too often get themselves hopelessly entangled. Sometimes they can't free themselves to live in harmony together. More often they can't free each other to separate or divorce amicably.

This is hardly surprising when we imagine the angry web of thoughts with which warring couples entangle each other.

One woman couldn't make a move towards her divorce. It was as though she was paralysed. And when she saw the cords, they were indeed immobilising her. She saw herself bound round and round with ropes, her arms pinned to her sides.

She evidently couldn't release herself so I asked who she wanted to come into her scene to cut the ropes. She chose Christ who entered her inner world and released her with great love.

Her husband was similarly bound round with ropes

and she then set to with a will to free him. He was quite happy to leave the inner scene and she burnt the cords with glee before she ran into a pool and rubbed and rubbed herself to get the circulation going again.

After the uncording in her inner world, she and her husband were able to co-operate to get the divorce moving and they were very soon released from each other in the outer world too.

Sometimes the cords are less obvious. One man saw himself and his wife covered in a spider's web. It exuded an unpleasant stickiness which had to be dissolved and washed away.

Once he had freed himself from the webbing, he could stand back and see the good points in the marriage. While he was fighting to free himself from the all enveloping stickiness, he had no energy to invest in the relationship.

Whenever we are negatively corded to anyone, whether to our boss or a friend of relative, it is helpful to take the golden spiritual scissors, then to visualise any cords and just snip them away with love. If someone is taking our energy, we snip the cord away, so that they can no longer drain us.

A very demanding young man sat in a healing circle in my house. He took all the attention so that no one else had the opportunity to contribute. It felt to me as if he was holding back the group and when I tuned in to ask for guidance, I was shown a curly cord and the golden spiritual scissors. I knew then that I was being instructed to release him.

For three days I sat down and visualised the cord which tied him to the group. I snipped the cord and imagined him leaving with love. On the fourth morning he phoned most apologetically. He hardly knew how to tell me but his job had called him away and he could no longer attend our circle on that evening each week. It was a powerful technique which should never be used lightly or thoughtlessly.

We can, of course, be corded to material possessions. If our house won't sell we are probably holding onto it and firmly corded to it. The same applies to cars, caravans, jewellery or anything we may wish to release.

When an old person seems to be hanging on to life, the greatest service we can do him is to check that we are not holding him back with our cords. We can unwittingly stop someone from going home by the emotional attachment we hold for them, positive or negative.

Whenever I've taken people through their chakras to check if there are any cords in them, they are invariably surprised at what they find. It is quite a simple exercise to do.

Visualise each chakra in turn, starting with the base chakra, which is red, and lies over the sexual area. See the chakra opening like a red flower. Go inside it. Clean it up if it needs it. Then relax and see what cords you can see coming from it. Follow each cord to see who is at the other end. Snip each cord with the golden spiritual scissors and release that person with love.

If a cord seems to be never ending and you can't find the person at the other end, demand that they make themselves known. It is your right.

Continue to do this exercise with each chakra in turn, like this. Visualise an orange flower in your abdomen, yellow in your solar plexus, green in your heart centre, light blue in your throat, indigo in your third eye, in the middle of your forehead and violet at the crown. When you are satisfied that each chakra is uncorded, close down the flower and seal each flower with a cross in a circle.

TWENTY-ONE

Responsibility

We are responsible for only one person in this life and that is ourself. At the same time individually and collectively we have a responsibility to every other human being.

When we take responsibility for another or let go of responsibility for ourself, we violate the Law of Self Responsibility.

The moment we take responsibility for someone else we are preventing that person from experiencing the lessons he needs to learn in this life. We are interfering with his karma and he may be unable to fulfil his life purpose because we took over an aspect of his life.

In order to lead a happy normal life a child needs to learn to walk. Naturally it is our responsibility to encourage and help him. If we don't want him to fall and get hurt, we hold his hand or carry him and this is appropriate in times of difficulty or danger. But if we hold his hand or carry him all the time, he will never be able to walk, run or climb independently or freely.

We have taken responsibility for his walking and stopped him from experiencing something important in his life.

No one would dream of doing this to a child and yet this is what so many of us do to others in life.

If we constantly prop someone up, emotionally, financially or in any way, we are taking responsibility for that person. If we feel we are responsible for someone's happiness or wellbeing or career or whatever, we must be aware of what we are doing. We are not letting them fulfil their karma.

We all undertake different lessons or experiences in life. Suppose, for example, that Ned needs to learn to handle money with wisdom as one of his life's lessons. However every time he gets into financial difficulties his father bails him out. Ned never has a real chance to take responsibility for his financial situation. He may never have the opportunity to learn his lessons about handling money because his father took responsibility for his finances. When he comes to review his life, will Ned thank his father?

If two people agree to climb a mountain and one carries the other all the way, neither benefits. The one who lets himself be carried has learnt nothing about mountain climbing. The one who 'nobly' carries his friend is preventing him from strengthening himself and from learning how to climb. He is also using so much of his own energy to carry the friend that he cannot fully experience the pathway himself.

There may be times when one or the other needs to be assisted or carried and then it is appropriate to help. We all need help at times.

Many an alcoholic leans on his wife. She feels she cannot leave him because he would go to pieces without her.

By propping him up she is making sure he never has the chance to work through his problems and take responsibility for his life.

If she refused to carry him through life, he would have the opportunity to learn to stand on his own two feet.

Pamela's husband was an alcoholic, a womaniser and he beat her regularly. He came to see me, a very charming, weak man, full of promises to make changes.

But he had no reason to change.

Pamela paid his debts, took him back when other women rejected him, submitted to his violence and generally supported him in his alcoholic addiction.

He cancelled or missed appointments and soon stopped coming. A few weeks later I had a call from Pamela in tears asking if she could see me. She was at her wits' end.

I talked to her about taking responsibility for another's life and she rocked back on her heels as if I had hit her.

All through her marriage she believed she had to support him. She believed that it was her duty, that she was doing the right thing for him.

She believed she was powerless to do anything else. She also hoped if she tried hard enough, he would change. She was taking responsibility for him changing!

Pamela went home and thought for hours. She realised she did have power, strength and courage. She told him she'd leave him if he did not stop drinking. She meant it.

She told him she would no longer bail him out financially. She meant it.

She told him that if he laid a finger on her again, she'd divorce him. She meant it.

He realised that she meant it all. He stopped drinking. Her act of courage forced him to take responsibility for his life.

Of course, he might have continued to drink. She would have left him and he could have gone to the gutter. That would have been his choice and his responsibility. He is responsible for what he does with his life.

The threat of suicide is an incredibly powerful manipulation and the would-be suicide is responsible for his own choice of life or death.

Carla had three brothers and sisters. Their mother tried to take responsibility for every one of their lives. Like an overwrought mother hen, she was carrying one grown up offspring up the mountain, then scurrying back for each of the others in turn.

Her whole life energy was devoted to running after them and taking care of their every need so that not one of those children knew how to look after himself. One became anorexic, another retired to a mental home and the other two tottered from one unsuccessful relationship to another.

Carla's life was a tangled mess and whenever she had a problem she would phone her mother for help. If her mother didn't come at once, Carla would threaten suicide.

Her brother and sister had already learnt that to

threaten to kill themselves was a powerful tool and used it constantly. The mother felt so responsible for them that she always responded.

She could not understand or accept that her grown up children were responsible for their own lives. She sacrificed her health, her finances, her life for those children and prevented each one from developing.

Because of her they were unable to experience and deal with the difficulties of life and so strengthen themselves to cope with greater tests. She did not allow them to climb the paths they had chosen for this life.

Carla came into therapy and very gradually strengthened herself and weaned herself from her mother.

She may or may not seriously have meant her threats of suicide. But the choice of suicide would have been her responsibility and no one else's.

We are each responsible for our own happiness.

It is often Mum who is the martyr in the family. Because at some level she believes she is not entitled to happiness, she places everyone else's happiness first.

When someone says, 'I only want my family to be happy. It doesn't matter about me', she inevitably has very low self esteem.

Because she places low value on herself, the resentment and fear simmer deep down inside her.

In negating and denying her right to happiness, she is expecting fulfilment second hand through her family. She is selfishly placing the burden for her happiness on the shoulders of her family.

Because she denies her needs and refuses to acknowledge even to herself that she has any, she can't ask honestly for what she does need. She may feel tired, hurt, angry, unloved or in pain but she can't express any of the feelings because she is denying herself and slaving away to make them happy.

Instead she expects the poor bewildered family to guess what she needs, to intuit what her feelings are, and respond.

When after all her efforts, they still aren't happy, she feels more worthless than ever and she buries her anger deeper. All her feelings of being unappreciated, underval-ued, all the tiredness and pain and hurt go out as an atmosphere around her. The whole family lives in the cloud of Mum's repressed feelings – and unconsciously she finds ways of taking out on them what she con-sciously denies.

When Mum values herself enough to take responsibil-ity for her own happiness, she finds ways of doing what she likes. She finds time for herself. She expresses her needs honestly, so the family no longer has to try to guess what she wants. It lifts a cloud from them. What a relief! The whole family can relax round her and be happy.

We are responsible for our own feelings

If we can't honestly express our feelings and thoughts to someone for fear of hurting that person, we are taking responsibility for his feelings.

We let failing relationships drag miserably on because we want to protect our partner. The truth is, of course, he has been picking up subliminally that we are withdraw-ing emotionally from him and that is far more destructive than a clean honest ending.

If we are saying to someone we love him and at the same time thinking that we're really fed up with him and want a new relationship, he is in turmoil and doesn't know what to believe.

Whether we pull the sticking plaster off slowly or quickly, he still experiences the pain. His hurt is his responsibility. It is part of his growth to deal with it appropriately by expressing the hurt, keeping his heart open and by learning the lessons from what has occurred.

I am not advocating that we deliberately hurt others. I am saying that when we are open and honest and take responsibility for expressing our feelings truthfully, we clear away confusion in other's minds.

It is often the easy path to protect someone's feelings. Most families collude to protect each other from hurt and it doesn't help their growth process.

Richard and Ann had been married for twenty years and did everything together. Richard became interested in wine tasting and a friend asked him to go on a wine tasting holiday. He very much wanted to go but he knew Ann would be devastated so he didn't dare even to mention it to her.

The wine tasting holiday was on his mind all the time. He felt really irritable and when Ann started talking about their annual holiday he snapped at her and then went quiet. Whenever Ann asked what was the matter, he replied, 'Nothing'.

He felt caged and raged inwardly that he couldn't do what he wanted. But he didn't say anything.

Ann obviously realised that something was wrong and was getting anxious. 'What isn't he telling me? Has he got cancer? Has he lost his job? Has he found another woman?' Thoughts began whirling in her mind. She became suspicious and overwrought, beginning to imagine all sorts of awful things.

Luckily Ann bumped into Richard's friend's wife, who mentioned what a pity it was that Richard couldn't go on the wine tasting holiday.

Ann's initial reaction was to feel anger because he hadn't mentioned it. She felt left out and hurt.

However she had done some self development work and had insights into herself and she realised that she was very dependent on Richard and had a great fear of being abandoned. She knew that she was terrified of Richard going away and leaving her.

So instead of rejecting the wine tasting holiday out of hand, she talked it over with a friend. After dinner she mentioned to Richard that she'd met his friend's wife and asked if he wanted to go on this holiday.

Richard was dumbfounded. 'Don't you mind? I thought you'd be terribly upset!'

Then they talked honestly. She told him of her fears and he expressed his frustration.

Ann recognised that she would imagine all sorts of things while Richard was away, so she decided to visit old friends during that week, who were delighted to see her. Once the intention was made the children organised themselves to stay with friends.

Richard felt the weight of the world lifting from his shoulders and he and Ann became closer than they had been for years.

While Richard was taking responsibility for Ann's feelings, the result was disastrous. If he had had the courage to express honestly what he wanted to do, a great deal of trouble and stress would have been avoided.

A lot of people say, 'It's alright for them. I'm different. It wouldn't work for me because. . .' and a whole string of excuses follows. And indeed they may be right but it only indicates that they have deeper work to do on themselves and their relationships.

Honesty can only help.

We try to protect children's feelings about their parents getting divorced by keeping silent and all the time their frightened faces tell the world that they know inside. Of course we are really protecting ourselves because we can't handle our own feelings.

Similarly when people haven't come to terms with death, they tell their children that someone has gone away or gone to heaven when they die and are not prepared to talk about it. They are cheating the children of a chance to express feelings because they daren't express their own.

The rage many children feel because a pet animal has been whisked away and disposed of while they are at school stays with them into adulthood.

Many of us who would never dream of cheating or lying to others will lie to ourselves and others about our feelings. We will suppress our true feelings (which is lying) under the guise of not hurting someone.

Thus, consciously and unconsciously we weave tangled webs.

We are responsible for our bodies and our sexuality.

Little girls take in many negative sexual messages, such as:

You've got to please your man or you'll lose him
If you get into trouble it's your fault

Nice girls don't
It's your duty
He needs it more than you
It's dirty
It's only to get children

And there are hundreds more. Small wonder that women carry in their consciousness a collective guilt and repression about sex.

Many women hand over responsibility for their body to their partner of the moment.

The pleasing, compliant girl will often extend this into becoming a pleasing compliant woman, who believes she doesn't have the right to say No, whether to a casual relationship or to her husband.

When we say to ourself, 'Oh no, not tonight', and still go ahead and have sex because he wants it, we are handing over responsibility for our sexuality. We shouldn't be surprised if we give ourselves cystitis or vaginitis or headaches.

I heard one woman complain, 'In all the years we were married, he never gave me an orgasm'. It's time she looked at her sexual blocks instead of blaming another.

Our sexuality is our power and both men and women for different reasons, give their power away.

We are responsible for everything in our lives. When we blame and criticise, we hand over our responsibility to someone else. When we say, 'He gives me a pain in the neck,' we are blaming him. When we say, 'I get a pain in the neck when he's with me. How am I giving him the power to upset me?' we are taking responsibility. No one can give us a pain in our neck. We give it to ourselves.

And what we are responsible for, we can change.

TWENTY-TWO

Depression

Our natural state is to have masses of energy running through us all the time. Loving, generous, happy thoughts keep our channels open and allow energy to flow freely.

Negative feelings such as anger, grief, jealousy block our channels. Anxiety and worry use a great deal of energy.

When our energy is totally blocked, we feel tired, listless, helpless and hopeless. We are open to heavy, morbid, gloomy thoughts and go into depression. The darker our energy, the heavier we feel and the more black our aura.

When we are faced with a great many problems or stresses, or have gone through a bereavement, our problems are visible, so if we become depressed, everyone says, 'It's no wonder. Just look what he's got to cope with.' People offer help and understanding.

When the problems are faced, the stresses cleared or the bereavement feelings expressed and healed, then vitality and energy flow and hope returns.

This depression is like seeing a mountain of rubbish which we know we have to clear away. It is visible for all to see and the more help we accept the more quickly it clears.

It is much more difficult when the rubbish is all covered up and hidden from view.

I saw a large pond once where the water seemed clear but the bottom of the pond was thick mud. Into the pond had been thrown bedsteads and bicycles, old boots and all kinds of rubbish. It all disappeared beneath the mud, leaving no trace on the surface.

However the rubbish was still there. It was no different from the visible rubbish. It still needed to be cleared.

So the person who represses feelings also goes into depression but his problems are covered up. People often don't know how to help because they can't see where or what the problem is.

The person who buries grief feelings has thrown a time bomb into the pond to lurk beneath the mud.

Life circumstances may cause an upheaval in the mud, causing a piece of rubbish to be uncovered. If we are too terrified to look at what's come up, we rush to the doctor for drugs. These gently heap a little more mud over the problem so that it sinks from view again.

Just because our problems are not visible it doesn't mean they aren't there. Drugs mask the symptoms by closing down our psychic centres so that the problem is inside us but cut off. They never clear away the cause.

Depression is saying that it is safer to let things hide under this blanket of mud than to face what is lurking there.

We are given opportunities through life to face the truth. Those times of upheaval are opportunities to grow. It is our choice whether to face with honesty or to deny. But whether in this life or another the clearance will have to take place. Once cleared each piece of rubbish is gone for all time.

When our own individual pond is cleared, everyone can enjoy it. So what we do for ourselves is an offering to everyone.

Olive's whole life was like a muddy turbulent pond. Her gloomy thoughts went round and round. She was beset by one problem after another. She never found time to stand back and let the mud settle to give her a chance to see clearly and take decisions to make changes.

Olive's parents put her into care as a small child, then flitted to another country and nothing was heard from them for several years. At the age of eight, little Olive was fetched to join them.

The child was terrified of leaving the only warmth and security she had ever known and of going to live with strangers in a seemingly hostile country.

Two qualities saw her through, prettiness and compliance. She cultivated both. Inwardly, she was a seething mess of rage and terror. She knew she must be really bad inside or else her parents would never have left her in the first place. She would do anything to please them, especially her father so that she wouldn't be rejected again.

At nineteen she fell wildly in love with a man while she was on holiday. They enjoyed a whirlwind romance and married within a few weeks. Olive fell pregnant immediately and was overjoyed. At last there was someone she could love who was truly hers and could never be taken away. She went to visit her parents and to tell them the good news.

When she returned to her husband, he had disappeared. In due course she discovered that he was already married. In her grief, Olive's solace was to live for the baby.

However, she had no means of support. Fate had confirmed her belief in her badness. She felt humiliated, tainted and sinful. The child was now illegitimate and when her father brought pressure to bear on her to have the baby adopted, she felt powerless. She buried her feelings and complied with his wishes.

It was almost inevitable that she should later marry a fickle, violent alcoholic who couldn't keep a job. She felt helpless to do anything about her husband's drinking and violence.

Her husband was invariably jobless or in prison and Olive struggled to bring up her children and make ends meet. For years her life ground on through difficulty and disaster because she could never take a positive decision. Her inward rage against her parents, her husband and life was enormous. And still she smiled on the surface and complied.

When it all got too much she retired into depression. Friends rallied round to cope with the children and help bail her out financially.

The only light in her life was when her mother died and left her almost enough to put a deposit down on a little cottage. She slaved to make the money up for that deposit. It wasn't until her husband stole the nest egg and gambled it away that she gathered strength and threw him out. Even after that, she bailed him out financially whenever he cried for help.

Problems still beset her as a one parent family and she couldn't cope or see a way out, so she slid down into depression again.

Despite the chaos and poverty she created around her, Olive was a very aware, very wise, well read and intelligent woman. In her smooth moments, she could see how she created the problems. She also recognised her great need of them. If there were no turbulence, no battles, no disasters, no fighting for survival, she would have to stop and face the terrible truth of her emptiness.

Now like many depressives, Olive was a sensitive. This means she was open to atmospheres, moon phases, weather conditions, people's moods and subtle energies all of which could affect her and alter her mood.

Lurking around her were the negative thought clouds of anger and frustration she had created. Other negative thought forms were attracted to her darkness. And during her low times, when life felt intolerable, she drank so that she opened up her psychic centres wide. All the negativity lurking around her was able to enter.

When we open up psychically we open up to our other lives and Olive had, like so many of us, had a black life. During her depressions, these memories flooded into her consciousness as living nightmares. Her depressions were hell.

Olive did make some decisions over time. Most importantly she decided never to bail her ex-husband out again in any circumstances whatsoever. She strengthened herself against the demands of her father.

She started to study to earn a qualification. That is both disciplining her mind and giving her some sense of self worth and of hope for the future.

Like all people who believe themselves powerless she

has used her power very effectively to create a miserable life and she is now starting to channel that energy to attract good things. When I last spoke to her she had found a home for herself and her children. She had found a steady job and was stabilizing financially.

She knows that she has the power to attract good into her life as well as disaster and is turning her energy around. She knows the warning signs of depression and has enough within her now so that she can keep it away. She knows she need never sink into depression again.

The basic cause of depression is that our energy becomes too dark and heavy and swamps the lightness.

Some people let their energy get heavy because of their thoughts about their personal problems, buried or obvious. Others are open and sensitive and are picking up heavy energy from the collective. They are transformers of collective negativity.

Most depressives do a bit of both of these things. So it is especially important to keep balanced with food, exercise, mixing with positive people, to raise the consciousness and to allow laughter and light in.

Brian was a very nice man in his forties. He was warm and caring and thoughtful and gentle. However a great deal of his energy was tied up in feelings of anxiety about himself and about life. He felt very insecure.

Brian passed through a period of depression lasting several months, only keeping his job because of the understanding support of his boss. He stabilised again and was in control on the surface but inside he felt close to tears most of the time. He felt very anxious with a permanent fuzzy head.

When he first came to see me he felt that the terrible depression could overwhelm him again at any moment.

On the positive side Brian took plenty of exercise and ate well, so that he was physically fit. He neither drank nor smoked and had a number of good friends. He loved his wife and children and the family was supportive. His job used his creative talents and he was good at it. So there were many things which were on his side.

Working against him were his lack of self esteem and his fear of life itself. He worried night and day about every little thing and used his powerful imagination to create difficult situations.

We worked together to strengthen his self confidence and self worth. As he became stronger inside himself he coped better and trusted himself to succeed in life.

Like Olive, Brian was a sensitive. He felt and responded to people's feelings to such an extent that he could be exhausted after being in a room full of people. Unknown to himself he was picking up their negativity and absorbing it.

He was a cleanser, which meant he had the special quality of being able to absorb other people's negative thought forms and cleansing their auras. And the act of doing so was exhausting him and putting him into depression.

Sensitivity is a gift. It means that we can be at one with other people because we tune in so acutely to their feelings that we become them.

The answer for Brian was to strengthen his self esteem even more. As he cleared more and more of his fears his aura naturally became stronger and brighter and therefore more protective for him.

It also helped him to use the golden coil visualisation. As many times a day as was necessary, he visualised a golden coil going around him from the ground up and opening up at his head. At the same time he thought or said, 'I am now totally protected from all lower thoughts and vibrations and open only to the highest'. Each time he visualised this and sent out the thought, he was setting in motion a protective force around himself.

Brian was beginning to feel very positive and in charge of life and then he woke one morning with the terrible unshakeable blanket of depression over him. He felt total doom and desperation. He found that even in the grip of the overwhelming despair, he was able to work out where it came from and shake it off within two days. It was a lesson for him. He realised that although there was a great deal more fear within himself to clear which could still all come up and attack him, he now had the power within himself to overcome it.

As Brian grows in strength and consciousness, he is becoming a powerful healer and cleanser and will be able to lift many others who are undergoing what he has experienced.

Nothing we go through is ever wasted

The hopelessness and helplessness of depression is an underlying factor in many illnesses.

Pauline was coming into her teens when her father left the family. Her dream had always been to marry and to have children of her own. Now suddenly her secure dream seemed dangerous.

Her mother's bitterness and rage at her father convinced her that relationships were not to be trusted. Before long Pauline's mother died and her world fell apart.

She retired into depression and became anorexic. Her mother's angry presence haunted her day and night until she was paralysed with fear.

It has been a long struggle out of a dark cold pit. In therapy she has seen a new perspective on her father and on her mother. She has strengthened herself against the overshadowing influence of her mother and has begun to take decisions.

Depression is like standing on an island in the middle of a muddy swamp. A decision to move in any direction means wading through unpleasantness and so it is easiest to stay where we are. However any movement at all in any direction is moving us towards the safety of dry land. So every decision, however small, is a step in the right direction.

There is hope. Pauline can get through her swamp and get to dry land. She can raise her consciousness and open up her energy channels and enjoy life. Recently she wrote this poem.

Cries of the Anorectic

'Tis an illness self-inflicted
There is no doubt;
Whereby one becomes addicted,
Doing without.
But that's too simple, there is more
A cry of help right from the core
Begging someone 'Open the door
Understand but don't ignore.'
Guide me God in finding the key
I am the Anorexia, and it is me.

'Tis anger, loneliness and fear
Which do torment
The price to pay, so very dear
On me I vent.
Struggles and battles in my head
Whilst I lie here confined to bed
Sometimes I wish that I were dead
These are the words I've often said.
Guide me God, what else can I be?
I am the Anorexia, and it is me.

But now darkness and me do part
Time to shine bright
For there's also love in my heart
This is my right.
I have been in a dreadful state
Much too thin and full of self-hate
Depart my fear and put on weight;
Find the light for it's not too late.
Thank you God for helping me see
It is the Anorexia, but not so me.

The deeper the depression, the greater the fear and so
naturally the more energy that is blocked. Blocked energy
can be released by physical exercise. As we walk in the
fresh air, the heavy energy starts to drain out of our feet.

When we say that a good walk raises our spirits, we are saying the same thing.

Putting on lively music and dancing is a wonderful way of raising the energy and dispelling negative clouds.

Doing things for others takes us out of our own cloud.

Blocked energy can be released by screaming out all those emotional feelings trapped in our tissues.

Blocked energy can be released by prayer and meditation, by raising our vibrations with chanting and reading inspirational works. Candles, flowers, incense, beautiful objects all raise our energies a little. All help us to open up to the power of Light.

A hug a day keeps depression away. When we are touched cuddled and held our bodies relax. We feel warmer and safer so that the fear locked in our tissues evaporates. The closeness validates us and makes us feel that whatever we do or feel we are still good enough for someone to want to hold us.

When we are in depression, we block out all hope, love and light. We are in our own living hell.

At present we put ill and depressed people together in hospital where the collective negativity of severely ill people often swamps the positive vibrations of the nursing staff.

People who suffer from depression are sensitive to emotions and feelings and atmospheres. How nice when mental hospitals and clinics are replaced by Healing Centres of peace and beauty where ill people can safely give vent to their most violently repressed feelings, can face and clear them and can raise their vibrations, surrounded by sensitives and healers who tune in to their needs and understand them.

If we are surrounded by hope, expectation of recovery and inspiration, then our minds are activated towards healing.

When people around us understand the spiritual Laws, we are open to absorbing their faith that mental, physical, spiritual and emotional blocks can be dissolved and healed by Love.

In their wisdom the ancients took people with depression to healing temples where they were spiritually lifted by consciousness-raising practises. At the same time the healing vibrations of the holy place entered their souls so that deep healing could take place.

TWENTY-THREE

Images and Affirmations

When we present our minds with the choice of logic or an image, the image will always win.

Place a wide plank on the ground and we will almost certainly be able to walk along it without a problem. Logic tells us that we can walk along that wide plank wherever it is.

However when we close our eyes and imagine the plank crossing a deep ravine, most of us have a fear response. Our imagination is stronger than cool logic.

This is the power of images and here are some ways of using imagery to help change what our logical minds cannot.

To switch off work

Many people cannot switch off from work. They come home from the office and their minds continue to churn. Logical thoughts about the pointlessness of the churning do not help.

If you are one such person, give yourself a few moments before you leave work or when you reach home.

Sit quietly with your eyes closed and let out a few deep breaths. Then imagine yourself throwing the papers from your desk into a briefcase and locking it away in an office cupboard or filing cabinet.

Then see yourself leave the office and stand outside watching the building shrink down to toy size. Place a black cloth over it.

If you do this regularly you are giving your mind a clear message to stop thinking about work when you leave the office.

One businessman found this exercise most effective. He told me with relish how he shovelled his secretary and colleagues into the cupboard, closed the door and turned the key on them!

He started sleeping properly for the first time in years.

The more emotional input we pour into our images, the more effective they are.

To free ourselves from unwanted influences

Visualise yourself sitting quietly on a peaceful golden beach and breathe gently. Watch an air balloon, bearing a huge basket float through the sky and land gently nearby.

Put into the basket all the people, things, or negative emotions you wish to clear from your life. Watch the air balloon rising up and floating away out of sight, carrying your rubbish.

If you are clearing an unwanted feeling or emotion, see yourself swimming in the sea after this. In this way you are symbolically cleansing yourself as well as expressing your freedom from the unwanted aspect of yourself.

When releasing a person from your life, it is often more appropriate to snip the binding cords with a pair of spiritual scissors, releasing them with love.

The Law of Non Attachment

Our Path is easier and happier when we aim for goals on route. A goal says that we know where we are going and of course both the aim and the direction can be flexible and can change.

If we are not attracting what we want it may be that we are attached to the outcome. In other words we set our goal, we aim for it and then we are unhappy if we don't achieve it. If non achievement of our goal makes us unhappy, we are attached to that goal.

So, having made our aim we must let it go by asking the Universal energy for the goal or for something better. After all the Universal Intelligence may have better and greater things in mind for us and while we are attached to our lower goal we block the higher aim.

So create the vision, expect to manifest it and let go of the having to have it.

The Law of Resistance

We get what we resist. So if we resist being poor, we get poverty. This is because when we resist something, we are fighting it. When we fight anything, the negative energy we send out comes straight back to us.

So if you are getting something you don't want in your life, are you resisting it? Accept it, then change your beliefs.

To reach a Goal

First we must decide on our goal. Many of us know vaguely that we want to succeed but the mind computer needs specific instructions. It responds to precise images.

If a man decided he wanted a house built but he couldn't make up his mind where or in what style and he wasn't sure how much he wanted to spend, so he just told the workmen to build him a house he could expect chaos. This is just the kind of vague thought instruction most of us give to our inner minds and then we wonder why things don't work for us.

So the man employs an architect and when he has a picture and plan and price for his house, he can delegate precisely all aspects of the work. He decides on the exact location and orientation and in due course the house is built according to the plan.

And when we want our life to go according to plan, we must make the same detailed decisions about what we want. We then breathe life into it with a clear image in our mind and feed it with positive thoughts. Then we let it go. In other words we let the workmen get on with the job of constructing our house and trust them to do it.

What we are doing is allowing our spirit guides and helpers and the universal energy to carry out our bidding and trusting them to do so. The only way it can fail is if we send out doubt or confusing instructions.

If you want a higher salary or profit, decide what you want and clearly image yourself receiving a cheque for that amount.

If you want to pass an exam, see the pass certificate with your name inscribed on it.

If you want to give a wonderful speech or performance, see yourself on the stage. hear the applause. Give yourself a standing ovation! Impress success into the very ether.

Then act as if you have already achieved your goal.

To attract the new

If we wish to attract something new into our life, for example a new house, we must do exactly the same thing. We must know precisely what we want.

First relax your body and empty your mind as much as possible of clutter. In other words make yourself available to listen to your inner wisdom.

Then write down exactly what you want. Make it reasonable and sensible but very optimistic.

If you want to move house, describe your new house in detail, including the layout, the location, the orientation, the size and the price. Bring it to life in your mind. Then visualise it in a pink bubble and release it into the Universe with the words, 'I ask for this or for something better for the highest good of all concerned.' Assume that the powers that be are working to produce your house for you and if it comes into your mind affirm positively that you are open and receptive to your new home.

As I was writing this chapter an ex-client phoned to say that I had taught her daughter this technique. Her daughter had recently moved to another part of England and imaged for a new house. She had seen the precise details that her daughter had written down and put into her pink bubble. She had just come back from her first visit to her daughter and had been quite shaken to see that the house was exactly as she had imaged, even to the type of tree in the front garden.

It is a powerful technique. Be absolutely certain you know what you want before you use it. If you decide you want a relationship, be certain that you are ready for what you get.

I decided that I was ready for a relationship and, after deep meditation, wrote down exactly what sort of a man I wanted. I wrote down the day our relationship would start.

On that day I started a relationship with a man. It was the right man but I wouldn't believe it. I doubted. I mistrusted. I put walls up and pushed him away, even though he was exactly what I imaged for, even though we had deep karmic involvement from other lives. It was over two years more before I released my walls sufficiently to realise that this was indeed the right partner for me. Then we were married.

There is a Law which says, 'Ask and you shall receive.' Inherent in this Law is the understanding that, having asked, we have total and absolute faith that we shall receive what we have asked for in a perfect way. We must act as if we have already received it.

The technique was perfect. The wisdom of the Universe was perfect. My little ego self was not ready and I did not have the necesary faith to accept.

If ever this method does not work for you, ask yourself why. Are you attached to the result? Are you resisting something? Are you impatient? Are you being prepared for greater things? Or do you lack the faith that what you asked for will come to you in a perfect way?

To find harmony within

Nature brings harmony to our being. Imagine yourself in a sunny valley filled with flowers, resting by a tinkling stream. Be very aware of the green grass and trees. Green is the colour of harmony. Absorb it.

Evoke the perfumes and sounds of the water flowing and birds singing. Be aware of the sun on your face and body and feel yourself growing in tune with the peace around you.

See the butterflies and leaves and hear the insects droning and bees humming.

The more you enter your inner world, the more deeply you can feel the harmony grow within you. When it becomes as real as if you were there, you are able to draw all you need from nature.

For strength

More and more people are becoming aware of the strength given out by trees. We can energise ourselves by leaning against certain trees and drawing in the power.

We do not have to physically find a tree. We can tune into their strength and energy by visualising a tree, imagining ourselves leaning against its trunk and opening up to allow the power to flow into us.

We should choose a tree in leaf or an evergreen for maximum effect but never an elm tree. Their vibrations do not harmonise with human vibrations.

Opening the heart

Many years ago when I was first learning about energies, a lady told me that when she meditated every evening, she visualised radiating pink light around herself. Recently, after she had given a talk a psychic approached her and told her that she was radiating a beautiful pink light.

I immediately realised that it would help me to visualise myself radiating light. At the time I was undergoing the trauma of divorce and knew I needed a strong colour, so I visualised a golden orange light flowing from my heart and surrounding me.

Two weeks later a stranger came up to me and told me I had a wonderful golden orange glow around me.

Pure love and wisdom is gold. To open your heart centre and experience your spiritual being, sit quietly and focus on your breathing. Imagine the golden flame of life in your chest.

Allow it to grow bigger and bigger until it fills your chest. Then allow it to grow bigger until it radiates around your body and you are in a complete golden cocoon.

Within a golden aura nothing and no-one can harm or hurt us. See the emotional brickbats that people throw towards you as arrows or daggers or bullets. Dissolve them in the golden light and see yourself returning them to whoever is throwing them, as little golden balls of love.

Sometimes we seem to be in the centre of a battlefield. *As long as we are radiating golden love, which is our armour of God, we can dissolve every attack and return it as love.*

The battle soon stops. *Love is a battle stopper – the only battle stopper.*

For protection

I find the golden coil visualisation very effective and it is quick and easy.

As many times a day as is necessary, visualise a golden coil of light going around you from the ground up and opening up at your head. At the same time think or say, 'I am now totally protected from all lower thoughts and vibrations and open only to the highest.'

Each time you visualise this and send out the thought, you are setting in motion a protective force around you which becomes stronger each time you use it.

Affirmations

Many of us spend much of our lives thinking fearful or angry thoughts or imagining the worst happening.

Each time we do this the negative beliefs that we hold in our minds are being reinforced and strengthened.

Affirmations are positive statements about ourselves. Each positive affirmation we make strengthens our positive beliefs about ourselves and stems the negative tide.

Sometimes we need to flood our minds with positive affirmations in order to turn the tide of our beliefs into a positive direction.

Anything with rhythm slips more easily into the mind, so a rhyme which can be easily chanted is very effective.

Singing affirmations also gives the words an energy so that they are absorbed by the mind.

The eyes are the windows of the soul so that statements made with eye to eye contact make a direct impact. This is why mirror work is so powerful. *When you say, think, chant or sing your positive affirmations directly into your eyes in a mirror, and do this with zest and energy you will be chasing away the old and imprinting the new.*

Here are some suggested affirmations.

Every cell of my body is filled with light
As I radiate Love by day and by night

I am divinely protected as I move forward with
Strength and courage and confidence.

Life is happy, life is fun
Life is dancing in the sun

Love, healing and wisdom flow through me
Touching others and setting them free

I now cast this fear from me
And hold God's hand as I go free

I give thanks that .... Is now manifesting for me in a perfect way.

I now attract the perfect relationship into my life

Good things keep on happening to me
I'm as happy and lucky as I can be

I feel good when I express my feelings and now allow myself to express what I feel.

I accept and love myself exactly as I am.

I allow abundance to flow into my life.

I am at one with my Higher Self.

I love myself and radiate love all round me.

TWENTY FOUR

Love and Light

Our creator is Love and Light. Love cannot create any-thing bad any more than Light can create darkness.

Because we were created by Love, we are love. It is our very essence. Darkness does not mean that the Light is not there. It means we deny the Light.

We come from light vibrations into the body for this testing experience on Earth.

Our purpose here is to manifest God within us – to recognise our God selves, in other words to recognise our divinity. *We are here to learn that we are not separate from God or each other.*

Before birth, when we choose our life pathway, we see the plan of what we can achieve. We know that our God selves can float through the difficult relationships, the bereavements, the hurts and rejections on the path, with love.

It is only our little ego selves which feel hurt, pain, threat and separation. Our aim is to release the ego self and our Higher Self will put us through almost anything to waken us to the realisation that we can let go.

We choose our life experiences, our links with people we meet, the pathway we follow, in order to put ourselves through the lessons and tests which we have not yet grasped.

It is difficult for most of us because we hold false beliefs. We believe that we are separate from God, that we are not Love, that we are impure and imperfect.

Each false belief causes fear and serves to show us that we are blocking out the Truth in some way. *So fear is our servant.*

Fear comes knocking at our door in the form of negative emotions, injuries, illness, traumas and difficulties. *Fear is, therefore, the servant which our Higher Self uses to waken us up from our soul sleep of ignorance.*

Every cell in our bodies knows the Truth of Light and Love. Light and love can never be hurt or injured. Only where we deny the Truth and impose a false belief on top of the light cells can we feel hurt. The truth is always there waiting to be revealed. So pain and illness are reminders to us to seek the illusion we are holding.

When Love shines brightly from our hearts and forms a golden aura around us, this is the armour of God. This is total protection.

When a crowd of children start school they are seen as a mass. They are the juniors and not too much is expected of them. As they get older everyone expects higher standards, greater sense and more discipline. The few who stand out will be noticed. They become prefects. All they say and do is noticed by their teachers, their peers and juniors. If they step out of line it will be observed.

In the same way much more is expected of an evolved soul.

If you feel you never get away with anything it may well be that your light is shining more clearly and you are being watched more carefully. More is expected of you. Some people have many more trials and difficulties to experience in life than others.

As children we used to learn the multiplication tables. They were drummed into us. We chanted them and were tested again and again. When our teachers knew we'd really learnt them by heart, the tests stopped. If we decide to go on to higher maths, we expect to be tested at a higher level. So it is with the hierarchy of souls.

An experienced soul is more rigorously tried and tested to make sure the lessons are in his heart.

And if a person wishes to progress, the tests will become progressively more difficult. The rewards and responsibilities greater.

If we float down a river in a canoe, we may choose to paddle comfortably in the shallows.

However, if we really want to explore the river we have to strengthen our muscles, refine our skills, learn to take white water and to paddle through jagged rocks.

When we've been tried and tested we may be chosen to join the training team. We are expected to be strong, reliable and dedicated.

And so it is with life. We can choose to stay in the shallows but we won't progress very far. To move forward we must be able to deal with difficulties with confidence. Other people's progression will depend on us.

The person who is getting away with things is building a backlog of karmic debts which will have to be repaid in due course. If we never get away with anything we should take heart. We are subject to Instant Karma. In other words our balance sheet of good and bad debts is being kept clear and up to date. All bad things are drawn instantly to our attention. It means we are on our way to higher things.

The more advanced our consciousness the more sensitive we are likely to be to atmospheres and to other's feelings. Negative things will register more quickly in the body, so we may suffer from ill health where an insensitive person would not.

It is frustrating when we feel we've really released a fear and then something much deeper comes up. Naturally it needs much more work to clear it or it wouldn't have lurked so deeply within. Take encouragement for many old souls are being given opportunities to clear from many lives and at deeper levels.

Many souls are choosing to be born now because of the great opportunities to experience, learn and develop at this time on the planet. We are in a time of great growth and change.

We come into incarnation with latent problems to work on and they may not be triggered until later in life. An event or place or a meeting can trigger an old memory which brings an awareness or feeling to the surface. Reaching a certain age can trigger soul memories.

A client suddenly developed asthma in his twenties. There was no history of asthma in his family. When he started to work on himself he discovered that he had died of an asthma attack at twenty in another incarnation. He had held a false belief that his essence of Love could be smothered. That false belief was triggered again as asthma, so that he could learn the Truth this time.

Because of travel, meeting more people, television and mass communications, more is being triggered within us. When we see someone on television we may have a soul recognition from another life. This can result in pain, rage, illness, phobia, anxiety – anything that reveals to us our opportunity to learn the lesson.

Of course soul memories can trigger wonderful things, latent talents and gifts, feelings of confidence and love. We can instantly have a rapport with someone and say, 'It's as if I've known her for ever.' We probably have.

A client said to me she couldn't help the mess she'd made of her life. It was her stars. Another told me a gypsy had forecast misfortune when she was fifty. Another had an unlucky name vibration under the science of numbers or numerology.

Of course all these things have a psychic influence. The thought once implanted has an even more powerful influence on the mind. The expectation of misfortune can create it. Our destiny lies within ourselves.

We are not victims. We do not have to be thrown around at random by the influences on us.

Psychic and mental influences can be dissolved by the spiritual, for Love dissolves all other influences totally. The Law of Karma is transcended by the Law of Grace, which includes the Law of Love and the Law of Forgiveness.

Once the Spriitual Laws are understood, the material things of life fall into their right place.

The Law says: As you give so you receive. So when someone sends out nastiness, it ricochets straight back and hits them. But when we absorb another's nastiness and radiate back love instead, the ricochet effect doesn't take place.

Someone says, 'How can I love a murderer?'

As we withhold love from the murderer we are judging.

When we set ourselves up to blame and condemn, we are acting from fear. Fear is the darkness within us.

When I started writing this book a terrible mass murder was committed. I heard about it on the news and mentally sent everyone, victims, murderer and bereaved alike, loving thoughts. When I went to bed I slept very deeply and woke with the sensation that I was being escorted back from a long journey and a door was shut behind me.

I had no dream but this was clearly impressed on my mind.

Those above who guide us were watching the rising level of violence and were aware that people were becoming increasingly disturbed by this. Yet nothing was being done and people felt powerless to do anything.

As a nation we needed a sharp lesson. The state of affairs had to be drawn to our attention in such a way as to make us stop, think and do something. The only way to do this was for something really shocking to happen.

The murderer and his victims had agreed to offer themselves to bring this lesson to the attention of the nation. They were all at the end of their chosen span for this lifetime. They could have chosen to die in accidents or by illness or in any number of ways. However their Higher Selves had consulted with the Higher Selves of all concerned and they had volunteered themselves for this purpose.

They were brought together at that time and place for the Plan.

I had the impression that this terrible tragedy to our earth eyes was a carefully orchestrated plan at a higher level to draw attention to the gun laws and to violence.

The shock wave from the tragedy moved people to action. As a result gun laws were tightened and gun owners became more careful. Violent scenes on television were curbed. People became aware of the seething feelings in the hearts of many loners.

The families received financial help which they would not have done had their loved ones died of illness or in accidents. The community drew together to console the bereaved families and each other.

I do not say that the impression I was given that night was right. Nor do I condone murder.

I do however believe that there is more that happens between Heaven and Earth than meets the eye. We see with Earth eyes and perspective.

So, who are we to judge? He who has never had a murderous thought may throw the first stone.

Some people accept the Spiritual Laws with an exclamation of wonder and delight. They are like walnuts ready and ripe to open at a tap.

Others feel knocked off centre when presented with Universal Truths. If our whole stability has been based on a dogma or 'ism' or rigid rules, it can be very threatening. We may no longer know who we are or what we stand for.

Those who feel threatened, become angry or throw ridicule or even threaten back, are reacting from fear. The fear lies within themselves.

Most cults or sects or religions have rules based on fear. If a sect says we must join them in order to be saved, that is a threat which comes from fear.

If a church says, 'You must not eat this, drink that, wear this, do that,' they are imposing controls. Whether the control is a sensible health precaution or an ego trip on the part of the leaders, it has nothing to do with spirituality.

Prohibitions are a threat. The implication is that if we do not obey, love will be withdrawn.

Some churches chant, 'We are miserable sinners. There is no health in us'. Chanting is a powerful way to slip messages into the mind, so these churches are persuading their congregations to open themselves to sin and ill health.

When we constantly infer to someone that they are bad, they come to believe in their own badness and act it out. The more we drum it in the worse they become.

Only love and acceptance dissolve the bad thoughts which we all have and allows us to grow and develop.

The rules of the Universe are based on love, harmony

and justice. I could add equality because everyone without exception is subject to the laws of love, harmony and justice.

There is only one Church. It is the Church of Love. There is only one religion. It is the religion of Love.

If we belong to a religion or sect which tells us we are bad, we can start asking, do we really need to be put down in this way.

If we belong to a group which leaves us feeling guilty, ask why. Why do they need to use fear? Then we can choose to join a group where we feel happy, peaceful, accepted and where the teachings are based on acceptance and love.

God is love. Therefore love is success, love is energy, love is health, love is joy, love is wisdom.

We teach what we most need to learn, so everything in this book is what I most need to learn. I am constantly doing things to myself and attracting experiences and people to myself in my quest to learn.

Knowledge comes from tuition. We can be taught facts. We can learn from books. But wisdom comes from intuition. It is within us.

I hope there are things in this book that intuitively strike a chord within you. If something is in accord with your inner wisdom, act on it.

Please choose Love and light up your life.

About the Author

Diana Cooper is a highly respected metaphysical writer, therapist, broadcaster and healer. She runs popular workshops in Britain and abroad and is the author of four books (all published by Piatkus): *A Time for Transformation, Light Up Your Life, The Power of Inner Peace* and *Transform Your Life*. Her work has helped thousands of people throughout the world.